FLORIDA KEYS
OVERSEAS HIGHWAY
TRAVEL GUIDE

101

BEST STOPS

ROAD TRIP FROM MIAMI TO KEY WEST
JUST SCAN QR CODE AND NAVIGATE
MARK WATSON

AUTHOR: MARK WATSON
GRAPHIC DESIGN: BART TROCH
EDITOR: RUSS L.
COPYRIGHT 2024
LOS ANGELES CA. U.S.A

THIS TRAVEL GUIDE BELONGS TO:

....

'IT'S THE BEST PLACE I'VE EVER BEEN ANY
TIME, ANYWHERE.'

ERNEST HEMINGWAY

DEDICATED TO ALL OVERSEAS HIGHWAY TRAVELERS FROM
AROUND THE WORLD

TABLE OF CONTENTS

INTRODUCTION

THIS TRAVEL GUIDE WAS CREATED TO HELP
YOU EXPLORE THE ROAD FROM MIAMI TO KEY
WEST AND EXPERIENCE AN UNFORGETTABLE
JOURNEY. YOU'LL DISCOVER THE TOP 101
DESTINATIONS ALONG THIS SCENIC ROUTE,
WITH HELPFUL REMINDERS TO ENSURE YOU
DON'T MISS ANY OF THE HIGHLIGHTS!

ARE YOU READY TO START YOUR JOURNEY?

RULES

This travel guide has rules that you must follow
to have fun and stay safe:

(1) This book conveniently lists all locations from Miami
Beach to Key West in the order they appear on the
road, enabling you to explore the area easily and visit
each destination.

(2) Before you start, plan your route. Consider the amount
of time you have to travel. Then select the places that
seem most interesting to you. If you would like to visit
a particular stop during your journey, be sure to mark
"TO VISIT" at the top left corner of the page.

(3) 30 stops out of the 101 included in this travel guide
are marked "Iconic Place." Keep a close eye out for
those! If you have limited time for your trip (no more
than 1-4 days), I suggest you limit your travel to only
these locations. Visiting all the points in this book will
take approximately 8-10 days.

(4) You can navigate to each destination by scanning the
QR code with your smartphone, using the included GPS
coordinates, or inputting the address into your navigation
system of choice.

RULES

---

(5) Remember, on some sections of the Overseas Highway you will be offline with no access to cellular data. The best way to navigate in these sections is with a standard GPS unit by using the GPS coordinates.

(6) Every time you visit a location, remember to check "VISITED" at the top left corner of the page.

(7) Don't forget to complete the travel journal each day. This can be found at the end of the guide.

(8) To make your journey easier, this travel guide includes easy to follow maps.

(9) The destinations were objectively selected by the author as the most interesting. However, do not be afraid to add your own stops if another place catches your interest. The selection of places for this book was not influenced by any financial contributions for promotion.

(10) The travel guide also contains a list of recommended lodgings and RV parks. In addition, speed limits are included. Follow the regulations and speed limits indicated on the road signs.

FREQUENTLY ASKED QUESTIONS

What and where is the Overseas Highway?

The Overseas Highway is a United States highway that connects the Florida Keys. It is a stretch of U.S. Route 1, which is the main north-south highway running along the East Coast. The Overseas Highway begins in Florida City, just south of Miami, and travels through Key Largo, Islamorada, Marathon, and finally reaches Key West, the southernmost city in the continental United States. The highway was originally built on the foundation of the Overseas Railroad, which was constructed by Henry Flagler in the early 20th century but was later converted into a highway after a hurricane damaged the railroad in 1935. Today, the Overseas Highway is a major tourist attraction and an iconic road trip destination.

How long is the Pacific Coast Highway?

The Overseas Highway is approximately 113 miles (182 kilometers) long. It extends from Florida City, just south of Miami, to Key West, the southernmost city in the continental United States. This scenic highway connects the various islands of the Florida Keys and is known for its picturesque views of the ocean, bridges, and tropical landscapes. In this travel guide, you will find a road trip that covers a total of 178 miles (286 kilometers), starting from Miami Beach and ending in Key West. The entire Overseas Highway is included in this amazing journey.

FREQUENTLY ASKED QUESTIONS

When to Drive the Overseas Highway?

The best time to drive the Overseas Highway is during the dry season, which typically runs from late November to mid-April. This period offers pleasant weather with lower chances of rain and hurricanes, making for a more enjoyable and safer driving experience.

Avoiding the hurricane season, which officially runs from June 1 to November 30, is crucial as the Florida Keys are susceptible to tropical storms and hurricanes during this time. Keep in mind that the peak of hurricane season is typically from August to October.

Therefore, the ideal time to drive the Overseas Highway is during the winter months when the weather is mild, and the risk of encountering severe storms is minimal. However, this is also the peak tourist season, so accommodations and attractions may be busier, and prices might be higher. If you prefer a quieter experience with fewer crowds, consider visiting during the shoulder seasons in late spring or early fall.

Always check current weather forecasts and road conditions before embarking on your journey, as conditions can vary, and unexpected weather events can occur.

FREQUENTLY ASKED QUESTIONS

What are the Overseas Highway's different names?

It doesn't have many nicknames. It is often referred to simply by its primary name. However, some people may use informal names or nicknames to describe certain sections of the highway or its overall character. Here are a few of those:

- Overseas Highway: This is the official name of the highway and the most commonly used term to refer to the entire route.
- U.S. Route 1: The Overseas Highway is part of U.S. Route 1, a major north-south highway that runs along the East Coast of the United States.
- Highway to the Tropics: This nickname reflects the highway's scenic route through the tropical landscapes of the Florida Keys.
- Highway That Goes to Sea: This nickname emphasizes the fact that the Overseas Highway extends over the water and connects a series of islands.
- Road to Key West: Since the highway leads to the southernmost point in the continental United States, Key West, it is sometimes referred to as the "Road to Key West."

How long does it take to drive the entire Overseas Highway?

Driving non-stop, it takes around 3 hours to travel from Florida City, FL to Key West, FL via the Overseas Highway. However, it's unlikely anyone would choose to travel this glorious road without any stops!

FREQUENTLY ASKED QUESTIONS

How long does it take to drive the entire route described in this guide?

The travel duration from Miami Beach, FL, to Key West, FL, via the Overseas Highway is approximately 4-5 hours without any stops. However, most will prefer to make several stops along the way. Generally, a trip covering only the main tourist attractions can be completed in 1 to 4 days. If you intend to explore all 101 destination points outlined in this guide, plan for a journey lasting approximately 8-10 days.

How long does it take to drive the entire route described in this guide?

Yes, there are tolls on some parts of the Overseas Highway. The tolls help fund the maintenance and improvements of the bridges and roadways. Make sure to have some cash or a SunPass for seamless passage through toll booths.

Are there accommodations along the Overseas Highway?

Yes, there are plenty of accommodations along the route, ranging from hotels and resorts to campgrounds. It's advisable to book accommodations in advance, especially during peak tourist seasons, to ensure availability.

FREQUENTLY ASKED QUESTIONS

Are there any restrictions for large vehicles or RVs on the Overseas Highway?

While large vehicles and RVs are allowed on the Overseas Highway, some areas may have restrictions due to narrow lanes or low bridges. It's crucial for drivers of oversized vehicles to check for any limitations and plan their route accordingly.

Is there public transportation available along the Overseas Highway?

Public transportation options are limited. Most travelers prefer to drive or rent a car to explore the Overseas Highway and its attractions. Taxis and rideshare services are available in some areas.

Is it safe to drive on the Overseas Highway?

Yes, it is safe to drive on the Overseas Highway. The route is well-maintained and safety measures are in place. However, like any other roadway, it's important to exercise caution, adhere to speed limits, and be mindful of other drivers. Additionally, staying updated on weather and road conditions is advisable, especially during hurricane season. Overall, with responsible driving and attention to local guidelines, the Overseas Highway offers a scenic and enjoyable journey.

DID YOU KNOW?

The Overseas Highway is a 113-mile (182 km) highway that connects the Florida Keys, running from Key Largo to Key West.

One of the most iconic sections of the Overseas Highway is the Seven Mile Bridge, one of the longest bridges in the world. It connects Knight's Key to Little Duck Key.

Before being converted into a highway, the Overseas Highway was originally built on the foundation of the Overseas Railroad, which was destroyed by the Labor Day Hurricane of 1935.

The Overseas Highway is also known as "The Highway That Goes to Sea" and "The Road to Key West."

Traveling on the Overseas Highway feels like island-hopping, as the road crosses over 42 bridges and goes through 44 islands.

Near Islamorada, there is a memorial called the Hurricane Monument, dedicated to the hundreds of World War I veterans who lost their lives while building the original Overseas Railroad.

DID YOU KNOW?

Key West, the southernmost point of the continental United States, marks the end of the Overseas Highway.

The famous American author Ernest Hemingway lived in Key West during the 1930s.

Key West is often regarded as the birthplace of key lime pie, a popular Floridian dessert made with key lime juice, egg yolks, and sweetened condensed milk in a pie crust.

The Conch Republic playfully acquired its name during a humorous and symbolic secession from the United States in 1982. Frustrated by a U.S. Border Patrol blockade in the Florida Keys, Key West residents "declared war," swiftly surrendered, and humorously christened their newfound micronation as the Conch Republic, inspired by the locally abundant conch shells.

On the streets of Key West, there are freely wandering roosters, descendants of jungle fowl with roots tracing back to Cuba and the Caribbean islands

Miami Vice, the iconic television series, was filmed against the backdrop of the vibrant city of Miami and the scenic shores of Miami Beach.

HISTORY

IN THE EARLY 1900S, THE FLORIDA KEYS WERE PRIMARILY
ACCESSIBLE BY BOAT, LIMITING THE REGION'S DEVELOPMENT.
HENRY FLAGLER, A VISIONARY INDUSTRIALIST, INITIATED
THE CONSTRUCTION OF THE FLORIDA EAST COAST RAILWAY,
EXTENDING TOWARDS KEY WEST. HOWEVER, THE RAILROAD'S
OPERATION WAS SHORT-LIVED AS A DEVASTATING HURRICANE
IN 1935 DAMAGED LARGE SECTIONS OF THE TRACK.

AFTER THE RAILWAY'S DEMISE, THE FEDERAL GOVERNMENT
AND FLORIDA COLLABORATED ON AN AMBITIOUS PROJECT:
TRANSFORMING THE REMAINING INFRASTRUCTURE INTO AN
AUTOMOBILE HIGHWAY. THIS MARKED THE BIRTH OF THE
OVERSEAS HIGHWAY. THE CONSTRUCTION OF THIS HIGHWAY
PRESENTED CHALLENGES, ESPECIALLY IN TERMS OF THE
EXTENSIVE BRIDGE CONSTRUCTION REQUIRED OVER OPEN
WATER. DESPITE OBSTACLES, THE HIGHWAY WAS COMPLETED
AND OPENED IN 1938, FACILITATING EASIER ACCESS TO THE
KEYS AND BOOSTING TOURISM AND ECONOMIC DEVELOPMENT.

TODAY, THE OVERSEAS HIGHWAY STANDS AS A TESTAMENT
TO HUMAN ENGINEERING AND DETERMINATION, PROVIDING A
PICTURESQUE AND ICONIC ROUTE THROUGH THE TURQUOISE
WATERS OF THE FLORIDA KEYS. IT CONTINUES TO BE A VITAL
LIFELINE FOR THE RESIDENTS OF THE KEYS AND A BELOVED
SCENIC DRIVE FOR VISITORS FROM AROUND THE WORLD.

OVERSEAS HIGHWAY PLAYLIST

Overseas Highway
Playlist

There are many hours of exploration ahead on the Overseas Highway, so here is a playlist with the perfect songs to immerse you in the stunning vistas and coastal landscapes. The first part of the playlist sets the mood with songs that capture the iconic 80s Miami vibe, perfect for cruising through the Miami area. Transitioning into the heart of the Florida Keys, the next section features local artists and classic hits, offering a musical embrace of the region's rich culture. As you continue your journey, we've woven in laid-back atmospheric tunes and reggae beats, creating a soundtrack that complements the relaxed ambiance of the coastal drive. Finally, the playlist wraps up with new modern tracks, tailor-made for your beach chill-out moments. So sit back, crank up the volume, and let the music transport you on a journey you'll never forget. Just scan the QR code using your smartphone and enjoy.

**SCAN QR CODE
AND PLAY**

MILEAGE

MIAMI BEACH, FL TO:

Miami, FL .... 9 MI/15 KM

Homestead, FL .... 42 MI/68 KM

Florida City, FL .... 43 MI/69 KM

Key Largo, FL .... 71 MI/114 KM

Tavernier, FL .... 78 MI/126 KM

Plantation Key, FL .... 81 MI/130 KM

Islamorada, FL .... 88 MI/142 KM

Layton, FL .... 102 MI/164 KM

Duck Key, FL .... 109 MI/175 KM

Key Colony Beach, FL .... 117 MI/188 KM

Marathon, FL .... 118 MI/190 KM

Big Pine Key, FL .... 139 MI/224 KM

Little Torch Key, FL .... 142 MI/229 KM

Ramrod Key, FL .... 143 MI/230 KM

Summerland Key, FL .... 145 MI/233 KM

Cudjoe Key, FL .... 149 MI/240 KM

Upper Sugarloaf Key, FL .... 151 MI/243 KM

Lower Sugarloaf Key, FL .... 153 MI/246 KM

Big Coppitt Key, FL .... 160 MI/258 KM

Key Haven, FL .... 165 MI/266 KM

Stock Island, FL .... 167 MI/269 KM

Key West, FL .... 170 MI/274 KM

WELCOME TO
FLORIDA

STATE: FLORIDA CAPITAL: TALLAHASSEE LARGEST CITY: JACKSONVILLE STATEHOOD: MARCH 3, 1845 ABBREVIATION: FL MOTTO: IN GOD WE TRUST NICKNAMES: SUNSHINE STATE, PENINSULA STATE, AND EVERGLADE STATE

FLORIDA SPEED LIMITS

RURAL INTERSTATES	LIMITED ACCESS HIGHWAYS	ALL OTHER ROADS AND HIGHWAYS
SPEED LIMIT 70 MPH	**SPEED LIMIT 70** MPH	**SPEED LIMIT 55** MPH

MUNICIPAL AREAS	BUSINESS OR RESIDENTIAL	SCHOOL ZONES
SPEED LIMIT 30 MPH	**SPEED LIMIT 30** MPH	**SPEED LIMIT 20** MPH

SPEED LIMITS ARE CLEARLY POSTED ALONGSIDE ROADS AND HIGHWAYS ON SIGNS OR DISPLAY PANELS. THE MAXIMUM SPEED LIMIT IN FLORIDA IS 70 MPH (113 KM/H).

THE SPEED LIMIT ON THE OVERSEAS HIGHWAY IS GENERALLY BETWEEN 30 AND 55 MILES PER HOUR. THE MAXIMUM SPEED PEAKS AT 55 MPH ON THE BRIDGES AND 45-50 MPH ON THE ISLANDS. THE SPEED LIMIT IS LOWER WHEN IN TOWNS AND POPULATION CENTERS.

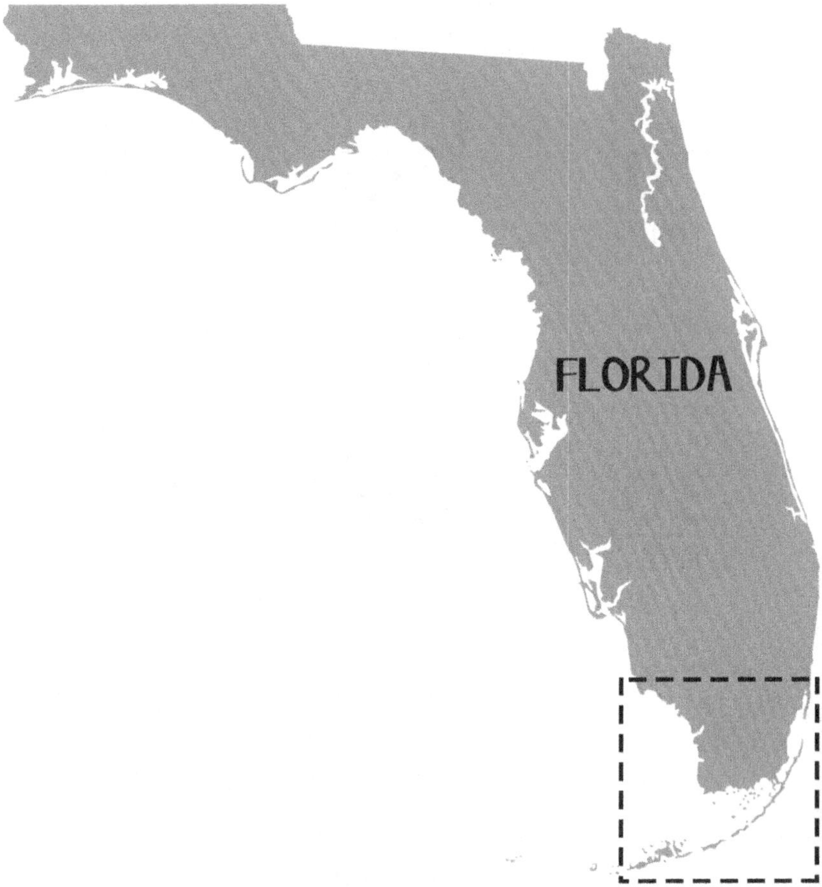
FLORIDA

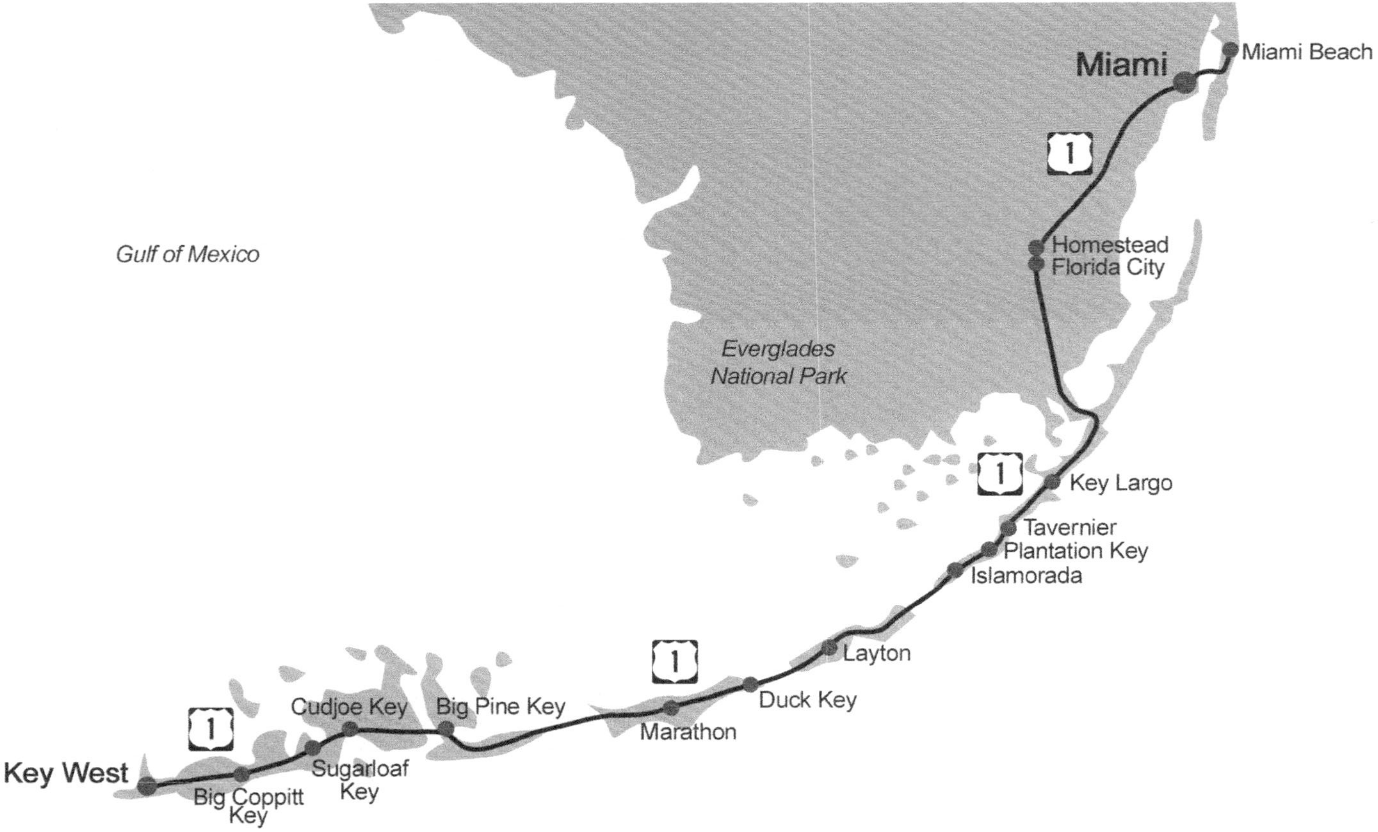
Miami Beach
Miami
1
Homestead
Florida City
Gulf of Mexico
Everglades
National Park
1
Key Largo
Tavernier
Plantation Key
Islamorada
Layton
1
Duck Key
Marathon
Big Pine Key
Cudjoe Key
1
Sugarloaf
Key
Key West
Big Coppitt
Key

'MIAMI IS ONE OF THESE GREAT PLACES THAT IS A REALLY
SENSUAL, PHYSICALLY BEAUTIFUL PLACE.'

MICHAEL MANN

WELCOME TO
MIAMI AREA

WHERE TO PARK YOUR RV IN THE MIAMI AREA:

This is a list of recommended RV Parks selected for a safe and comfortable stay:

RV PARKS

Yacht Haven Park & Marina
2323 W State Rd 84, Fort Lauderdale, FL 33312

CB Smith County Campground
1381 NW 129th Ave, Pembroke Pines, FL 33028

Embassy RV Park
3188 Lake Shore Dr, Hallandale Beach, FL 33009

Larry and Penny Thompson Memorial Park
12451 SW 184th St, Miami, FL 33177

Encore Miami Everglades
20675 SW 162nd Ave, Miami, FL 33187

Palm Garden RV Park
28300 SW 147th Ave, Homestead, FL 33033

Homestead Trailer Park
31 SE 2nd Rd, Homestead, FL 33030

Southern Comfort RV Resort
345 E Palm Dr, Florida City, FL 33034

Goldcoaster
34850 SW 187th Ave, Homestead, FL 33034

WHERE TO STAY IN THE MIAMI AREA:

APARTAMENTS

Pantera Rosa
2323 W State Rd 84, Fort Lauderdale, FL 33312

CB Smith County Campground
1415 Collins Avenue, Miami Beach, FL 33139

Nomada Destination Residences - Quadro
3900 Biscayne Blvd, Miami, FL 33137

Renzzi Wyndwood Apartments
856 NW 29th St, Miami, FL 33127

Private Oasis at Arya
2889 McFarlane Road, Coconut Grove, Miami, FL 33133

HOTELS

Eurostars Langford
121 Southeast 1st Street, Miami, FL 33131

YOTEL Miami
227 Northeast 2nd Street, Miami, FL 33132

The Elser Hotel Miami
398 Northeast 5th Street, Miami, FL 33132

Hotel AKA Brickell
1395 Brickell Ave, Miami, FL 33131

THesis Hotel Miami
1350 S. Dixie Highway, Coral Gables, Miami, FL 33146

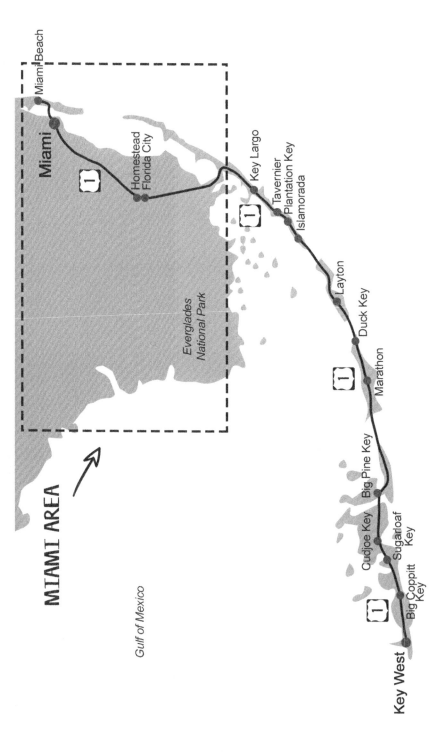

PLACES TO VISIT IN
THE MIAMI AREA:

(1) North Beach Oceanside Park

(2) Miami Beach

(3) Carlyle Cafe

(4) Art Deco Welcome Center

(5) Ocean Drive

(6) Wynwood Walls

(7) Phillip & Patricia Frost Museum of Science

(8) Freedom Tower

(9) Bayside Marketplace

(10) Skyviews Miami Observation Wheel

(11) Vizcaya Museum & Gardens

(12) Bayshore Club

(13) Mr. Bean

(14) Cauley Square Historic Village

(15) Coral Castle

(16) Historic Town Hall of Homestead

(17) Robert Is Here Fruit Stand

(18) Everglades National Park

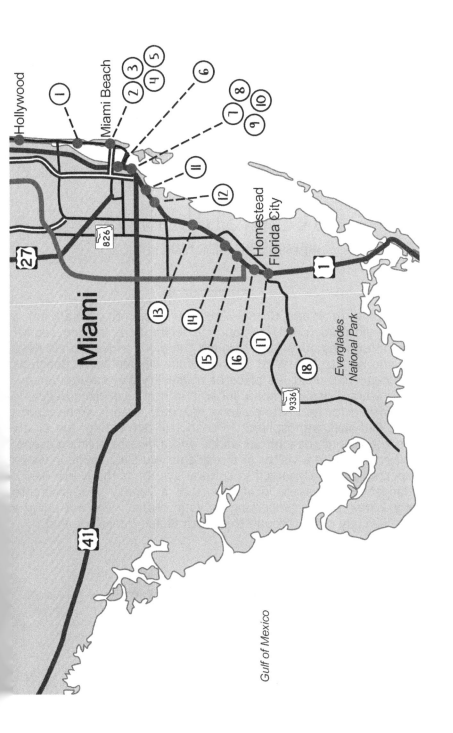

☐ TO VISIT
☐ VISITED

NORTH BEACH OCEANSIDE PARK

MILEAGE: 0 MI/ 0 KM MIAMI BEACH, FL

25.86839, -80.12051

Welcome to Miami Beach! Are you ready to embark on a 178-mile road trip? Your journey begins here, as you set off on an exciting adventure through the picturesque Florida Keys all the way to Key West. I've carefully chosen North Beach as your starting point – a place of tranquility and natural beauty. This vibrant neighborhood, located in northern Miami Beach, is renowned for its pristine sandy beaches, historic architecture, and laid-back atmosphere. It boasts a captivating mix of art deco buildings, beachfront parks, and a diverse culinary scene. Whether you're a visitor or a resident, you can indulge in water sports, immerse yourself in cultural events at the North Beach Bandshell, and savor local flavors at a variety of restaurants and cafes. Before embarking on your journey, why not enjoy a leisurely stroll through the North Beach Oceanside Park?

North Beach Oceanside Park
8328 Collins Ave, Miami Beach, FL 33141

**SCAN QR CODE
TO NAVIGATE**

02

ICONIC PLACE

NATURAL LANDMARK

MIAMI BEACH

MILEAGE: 5 MI/ 8 KM MIAMI BEACH, FL

25.80035, -80.12488

Ever envisioned lounging and sunbathing on the expansive sandy shores of Miami Beach? Interestingly, much of that sand is not native to the area. Local authorities import a portion of it from the Caribbean, with the Bahamas being a common source. In 2017, authorities undertook a massive effort to combat erosion by replenishing Mid-Beach with a staggering 285,412 tons of sand, at a cost of approximately $11.5 million to the state of Florida. Let's head to the beach and soak up some sun. As you step onto the warm sands of Miami Beach, you'll be greeted by the rhythmic sound of the ocean waves and the gentle caress of the sea breeze. The beach stretches for miles, providing ample space for sunbathers, swimmers, and water sports enthusiasts. It's a haven for beachgoers seeking a sun-kissed escape.

Miami Beach
1000 Miami Beach Dr, Miami Beach, FL 33139

**SCAN QR CODE
TO NAVIGATE**

03

CAFE

THE CARLYLE

MILEAGE: 6 MI/ 10 KM MIAMI BEACH, FL
25.78382, -80.13010

The Carlyle, a renowned Art Deco gem, is a historic and iconic hotel nestled in the heart of Miami Beach. This architectural masterpiece stands as a testament to the glamour and sophistication of a bygone era. Situated in the vibrant South Beach neighborhood, The Carlyle has been a beloved fixture on the Miami Beach scene for decades. The Carlyle is a visual delight, boasting the signature pastel hues and intricate geometric patterns that define the Art Deco style. Its striking facade and elegant interiors transport guests to a time when Miami Beach was emerging as a hub of luxury and entertainment. Notably, The Carlyle was featured in the popular TV series "Miami Vice," which added to its cultural significance. In the show, Sonny Crockett and Rico Tubbs frequently visited this cafe, giving it a memorable place in the annals of Miami Vice history. Whether you're planning a one-night stay, wish to explore the Art Deco architecture, or yearn to step into the shoes of Crockett and Tubbs while savoring a coffee, The Carlyle is a place that definitely merits a visit.

Carlyle Cafe
1250 Ocean Dr, Miami Beach, FL 33139

**SCAN QR CODE
TO NAVIGATE**

TO VISIT
VISITED

04

TOURIST ATTRACTION

ART DECO WELCOME CENTER
MILEAGE: 7 MI/ 11 KM MIAMI BEACH, FL
25.78029, -80.13045

Let's shift gears and visit the Art Deco Welcome Center, a cultural and historical hub situated in the heart of the city's iconic Art Deco Historic District. Housed in a building that's a striking example of the style, the center serves as a gateway for visitors and a resource for those interested in the area's architectural heritage. The center offers a wealth of information about the district's distinctive architecture and history, making it a must-visit for architecture enthusiasts. It provides walking tours that explore the beautifully preserved buildings and their unique design elements. Additionally, the center hosts events, exhibitions, and educational programs that celebrate the Art Deco legacy of Miami Beach.

Art Deco Welcome Center
1001 Ocean Dr, Miami Beach, FL 33139

**SCAN QR CODE
TO NAVIGATE**

05

ICONIC PLACE

TOURIST ATTRACTION

OCEAN DRIVE

MILEAGE: 8 MI/ 13 KM MIAMI BEACH, FL

25.76851, -80.13320

It's time to immerse yourself in the Art Deco style and take a ride along the coast via the renowned Ocean Drive! Lined with pastel-colored, meticulously preserved Art Deco buildings, Ocean Drive is a visual feast and a testament to Miami Beach's architectural heritage. The neon lights that illuminate the street in the evening create a mesmerizing and electric ambiance, making this a popular spot for nighttime entertainment. The street is also home to a myriad of restaurants, cafes, bars, and boutique shops, offering a prime destination for dining, people-watching, and shopping. The outdoor seating at many establishments allows you to savor your meal or drinks while enjoying the ocean breeze and the lively street scene.

Ocean Dr
Ocean Dr, Miami Beach, FL 33139

**SCAN QR CODE
TO NAVIGATE**

06

ICONIC
PLACE

TOURIST
ATTRACTION

WYNWOOD WALLS

MILEAGE: 12 MI/ 19 KM MIAMI, FL
25.80084, -80.19933

Welcome to Miami! Remarkably, Miami is the only major U.S. city in history to have been founded by a woman. Often heralded as the 'Mother of Miami,' Julia Tuttle was a local businesswoman who owned property in the area. She played a pivotal role in convincing the railway magnate, Henry Flagler, to extend the railroad into the Miami River territory. In an extraordinary gesture, she offered him land for a hotel and a railroad station, completely free of charge. On April 22, 1896, the railway finally reached its destination, and in July of the same year, the city's 28 residents came together to officially incorporate the city. The city's name, Miami, pays homage to the Mayaimi, an indigenous tribe that inhabited the region during the 17th and 18th centuries. To begin your visit in Miami, I recommend starting at Wynwood Walls, a renowned outdoor art gallery located in the Wynwood Arts District. This vibrant and dynamic space is adorned with colorful and captivating street art, murals, and graffiti created by local and international artists. Undoubtedly a visit worth making!

Wynwood Walls
2516 NW 2nd Ave, Miami, FL 33127

**SCAN QR CODE
TO NAVIGATE**

07

PHILLIP & PATRICIA FROST
MUSEUM OF SCIENCE

MILEAGE: 13 MI/ 21 KM MIAMI, FL
25.78525, -80.18791

Your next destination should undoubtedly be the Phillip and Patricia Frost Museum of Science. Named in honor of its generous benefactors, Dr. Phillip Frost and Patricia Frost, this museum is a regional beacon of scientific exploration and education. This awe-inspiring institution offers a fascinating journey into the world of science and discovery. Opened in 2017, the museum features a stunning architectural design that combines modern aesthetics with ecological considerations, making it a visual landmark in the city. The museum's mission is to inspire a passion for science, encourage curiosity, and promote understanding of the natural world. It achieves this by offering an array of engaging exhibits and interactive experiences across various disciplines, from astronomy and physics to biology and environmental science.

Phillip & Patricia Frost Museum of Science
1101 Biscayne Blvd, Miami, FL 33132

**SCAN QR CODE
TO NAVIGATE**

08

TOURIST
ATTRACTION

FREEDOM TOWER
MILEAGE: 14 MI/ 23 KM MIAMI, FL
25.78033, -80.18943

The Freedom Tower is a historic landmark and a symbol of Cuban immigration to the United States. Listed on the National Register of Historic Places, the tower's architecture is inspired by the Giralda Tower of the Cathedral of Seville in Spain and features a Mediterranean Revival design. It was originally constructed in 1925 as the headquarters for The Miami News, a prominent newspaper at the time. In the 1960s, it was repurposed as an immigration processing center for Cuban refugees fleeing the Fidel Castro regime. Many Cuban exiles were processed through this building, making it an important symbol of their search for freedom. In addition to its historical significance, the Freedom Tower now serves as a cultural center and museum, showcasing exhibitions related to Cuban immigration and Miami's diverse cultural heritage. It is also part of Miami Dade College and continues to be an important landmark in the city.

Freedom Tower at Miami Dade College
600 Biscayne Blvd, Miami, FL 33132

**SCAN QR CODE
TO NAVIGATE**

09

ICONIC
PLACE

TOURIST
ATTRACTION

BAYSIDE MARKETPLACE

MILEAGE: 14 MI/ 23 KM MIAMI, FL
25.77843, -80.18680

Nestled in the vibrant heart of Miami, Bayside Marketplace is a harmonious blend of shopping, dining, and entertainment, catering to visitors of all ages. This iconic destination features over 150 shops, boutiques, and kiosks, making it a shopaholic's paradise that meets every conceivable need and desire from trendy fashion to one-of-a-kind souvenirs. While some higher-end stores may appear a bit pricey, most are surprisingly affordable, ensuring an enjoyable shopping experience without breaking the bank. With numerous dining options offering a variety of cuisines, you can savor a delicious meal with a picturesque view of Biscayne Bay. Bayside Marketplace also hosts live entertainment, street performers, and cultural events, ensuring there's always something exciting happening. For those seeking adventure, boat tours along Biscayne Bay and stunning views of the Miami skyline are readily available. Whether you're looking to shop, dine, relax by the bay, or be entertained, Bayside Marketplace has it all, making it a must-visit destination in Miami.

Bayside Marketplace
401 Biscayne Blvd, Miami, FL 33132

**SCAN QR CODE
TO NAVIGATE**

SKYVIEWS MIAMI OBSERVATION WHEEL

MILEAGE: 14 MI/ 23 KM MIAMI, FL

25.77694, -80.18452

After visiting Bayside Market, I highly recommend taking a ride on the Skyviews Miami Observation Wheel conveniently located nearby. This towering observation wheel offers visitors a breathtaking experience as they soar above the city, providing panoramic views of the stunning Miami skyline, Biscayne Bay, and the surrounding area. Fun Fact: The Skyviews Miami Observation Wheel is one of the tallest observation wheels in the southeastern United States, standing at an impressive height of 176 feet (53.6 meters). It features 42 climate-controlled gondolas, ensuring a comfortable and memorable ride for guests.

Skyviews Miami Observation Wheel
401 Biscayne Blvd, Miami, FL 33132

**SCAN QR CODE
TO NAVIGATE**

VIZCAYA MUSEUM & GARDENS

MILEAGE: 17 MI/ 27 KM MIAMI. FL
25.74434, -80.21047

The Vizcaya Museum & Gardens, located in Miami, Florida, is a stunning and historic estate that offers a captivating blend of art, architecture, and lush greenery. Originally constructed as a winter residence for industrialist James Deering in the early 20th century, Vizcaya has since become a renowned cultural and historical landmark. The main attraction at Vizcaya is the opulent Italian Renaissance-style villa, which is a marvel of architecture and design. Visitors can explore the beautifully adorned rooms, each boasting intricate details, art, and period furnishings. The villa overlooks Biscayne Bay and offers breathtaking views of the water and surrounding gardens. The gardens at Vizcaya are a masterpiece of landscape design, featuring elegant fountains, sculptures, and a vast collection of rare and exotic plants. The lush greenery includes a variety of formal gardens such as the Italian Garden, the Secret Garden, and the Village Pool Garden, each boasting a unique charm.

Vizcaya Museum & Gardens
3251 S Miami Ave, Miami, FL 33129

**SCAN QR CODE
TO NAVIGATE**

BAYSHORE CLUB

MILEAGE: 20 MI/ 32 KM MIAMI, FL

25.72870, -80.23415

After spending the day exploring Miami, it's time to choose a great place for lunch or dinner. I highly recommend the Bayshore Club which offers fantastic views of Biscayne Bay and the nearby marina. They have an excellent selection of seafood and beverages. Located on the historic site of Dinner Key, the island served as the first continental naval air station in the United States during WWI. In the 1930s and 40s, it was a base for Pan American World Airways' flying boats (the Sikorsky S41 and S42). The restaurant is inspired by the golden age of flight, offering a nostalgic experience with a focus on pre-flight meals and the thrill of travel. After visiting Bayshore Club, continue your adventure by taking U.S. Route 1 to the next destination!

Bayshore Club
3391 Pan American Dr, Miami, FL 33133

**SCAN QR CODE
TO NAVIGATE**

MR. BEAN

MILEAGE: 29 MI/ 47 KM MIAMI, FL
25.64560, -80.34013

One of my favorite things during my adventures is discovering small, cozy cafes. As we continue our journey to Key West along U.S. Route 1, I have an excellent recommendation for all the fellow coffee aficionados out there: Mr. Bean! This charming café is conveniently located close to the main road. From a perfect cup of cappuccino to delectable croissants, the delightful range of treats at Mr. Bean doesn't disappoint. It's also an ideal spot to start your day with a scrumptious breakfast. As you step into Mr. Bean, you'll immediately sense its warm and welcoming ambiance. The aroma of freshly brewed coffee fills the air and the cozy seating areas make it an inviting place to relax. So, whether you're passing through or looking for a local gem, make sure to make a pitstop at Mr. Bean.

Mr. Bean
8888 SW 136th St Suite 585, Miami, FL 33176

**SCAN QR CODE
TO NAVIGATE**

HISTORICAL
LANDMARK

CAULEY SQUARE
HISTORIC VILLAGE

MILEAGE: 36 MI/ 58 KM MIAMI, FL

25.55866, -80.39060

We're gradually bidding farewell to Miami with our final stop on the southern outskirts of the city. Cauley Square Historic Village is a charming village showcasing classic chalets, gardens, shops, and dining options. Established in 1903 as Gould's Siding, later known as Goulds, Cauley Square Historic Village played a crucial role in shipping Redland's produce via Henry Flagler's railroad. Originally home to William Cauley's distinctive two-story warehouse and office, packing houses, living quarters, and even a saloon appeared as the area grew, giving Cauley Square a rowdy reputation. Over the years, it weathered storms and economic challenges, but by the mid-20th century, the village faced demolition. Mary Anne Ballard, an advocate of history and art, saw the potential in the main building and purchased it with the vision of restoring Cauley Square. She aimed to create a space for small businesses, dining, and arts and education centers. Today, Cauley Square remains a thriving hidden gem in South Florida, preserving a rich history and unique character.

Cauley Square Historic Village
22400 Old Dixie Hwy, Miami, FL 33170

**SCAN QR CODE
TO NAVIGATE**

15

CORAL CASTLE

MILEAGE: 41 MI/ 66 KM HOMESTEAD, FL

25.50055, -80.44445

Coral Castle is a fascinating and enigmatic structure located in Homestead. It is often referred to as one of the world's most mysterious and baffling architectural marvels due to the circumstances of its creation and the sheer scale of the undertaking by a single man. Built by a Latvian immigrant named Edward Leedskalnin, Coral Castle has captured the imaginations of many and has become a popular tourist attraction. One of the most astonishing aspects of Coral Castle is the mystery surrounding how the frail and unassuming Leedskalnin managed to accomplish this feat using only simple tools and his deep understanding of masonry. He left behind very few records or detailed explanations of his construction techniques, which led to a wide range of theories and speculation about how he achieved this incredible task. Some believe Leedskalnin possessed advanced knowledge of magnetism and anti-gravity, while others suggest that he used a combination of pulleys, levers, and counterweights. However, no definitive explanation has been agreed upon, adding to the mystique of Coral Castle.

Coral Castle
28655 S Dixie Hwy, Homestead, FL 33033

**SCAN QR CODE
TO NAVIGATE**

16

MUSEUM

HISTORIC TOWN HALL
OF HOMESTEAD
MILEAGE: 44 MI/ 71 KM HOMESTEAD, FL
25.47065, -80.47723

Welcome to Homestead, known for its agricultural history and its proximity to Everglades National Park. I highly recommend taking a leisurely stroll through the city's streets and visiting the Historic Town Hall of Homestead. The structure has historical significance and is a well-preserved example of Mediterranean Revival architecture. Constructed in 1917, it served as the city's government center for several decades. The building's architecture reflects the Mediterranean Revival style popular during the early 20th century in Florida. It features distinctive elements such as arched windows and doorways, red-tiled roofs, and stucco walls. Today, a museum beautifully showcases the history of Homestead and Florida. One of the most popular exhibits is the City of Homestead's original 1924 American LaFrance fire truck. Additionally, be sure not to overlook the beautiful clock out front.

Historic Town Hall of Homestead
41 N Krome Ave, Homestead, FL 33030

**SCAN QR CODE
TO NAVIGATE**

17

ICONIC PLACE

TOURIST ATTRACTION

ROBERT IS HERE FRUIT STAND

MILEAGE: 47 MI/ 76 KM HOMESTEAD, FL
25.44747, -80.50176

Nestled a mere 3 miles away from the heart of Homestead, the renowned destination awaits: Robert Is Here Fruit Stand. This charming locale, steeped in local allure, beckons both residents and wanderers alike to experience a cornucopia of flavors. Established by Robert Moehling, the stand has become a must-visit destination for all Miami - Key West travelers, offering a wide variety of delicious fruits, homemade jams, and other delectable treats. Robert Moehling started the business as a humble fruit stand when he was just 6 years old, instructed by his father to sell surplus cucumbers on the side of the road. By the time he was 14, young Robert bought 10 acres of land with a house, a car, and a lawnmower. Now, Robert boasts one of the most renowned fruit stand in Florida. Whether you're a local resident or a passing traveler, Robert Is Here Fruit Stand provides a delightful experience for all who appreciate high-quality, fresh produce.

Robert Is Here Fruit Stand
19200 SW 344th St, Homestead, FL 33034

**SCAN QR CODE
TO NAVIGATE**

TO VISIT
VISITED

18

 ICONIC PLACE

 NATURAL LANDMARK

 OFF THE MAIN ROUTE

EVERGLADES NATIONAL PARK
OFF THE MAIN ROUTE 8 MI / 13 KM
25.39531, -80.58304

Embark on a journey from Florida City, following the scenic State Road 9336, to discover one of the USA's most renowned national treasures - Everglades National Park. Spanning over 1.5 million acres, this UNESCO World Heritage Site is home to a diverse range of habitats, from sawgrass marshes to mangrove forests. For an immersive experience, many visitors opt for airboat tours, a popular and exhilarating way to explore the park's waterways. These guided tours provide a thrilling ride through the park's intricate maze of water channels, offering close encounters with resident alligators, diverse bird species, and other fascinating wildlife. The airboat tours not only showcase the park's natural beauty but also provide insights into the delicate balance of this ecosystem. If you'd like to begin your visit, I highly recommend starting from the Ernest F. Coe Visitor Center. It is about 8 miles (13 kilometers) away from the Robert is Here Fruit Stand.

Ernest F. Coe Visitor Center
40001 State Hwy 9336, Homestead, FL 33034

SCAN QR CODE TO NAVIGATE

'EVERY TIME I SLIP INTO THE OCEAN, IT'S LIKE GOING HOME.'

SYLVIA EARLE

WHERE TO PARK YOUR RV IN UPPER KEYS:

This is a list of recommended RV Parks selected for a safe and comfortable stay:

RV PARKS

Pelican Cay RV Park LLC
299 Morris Ave, Key Largo, FL 33037

Keys Palms RV Resort
104200 Overseas Hwy, Key Largo, FL 33037

Key Largo Kampground & Marina
101551 Overseas Hwy, Key Largo, FL 33037

Keys Ventures @ 101
101600 Overseas Hwy, Key Largo, FL 33037

Calusa Campground Resort & Marina
325 Calusa St, Key Largo, FL 33037

Blue Fin Rock Harbor RV Park & Marina
36 E 2nd St, Key Largo, FL 33037

Sun Outdoors Islamorada
87395 Old Hwy #1, Islamorada, FL 33036

WHERE TO STAY IN UPPER KEYS:

RESORTS/HOTELS

Gilbert's Resort
107900 Overseas Hwy, Key Largo, FL 33037

Reefhouse Resort & Marina
103800 Overseas Hwy Mm 103.8, Key Largo, FL 33037

Hampton Inn Key Largo, FL
102400 Overseas Hwy, Key Largo, FL 33037

Dolphin Point Villas
101910 Overseas Hwy, Key Largo, FL 33037

Baker's Cay Resort Key Largo
97000 Overseas Hwy, Key Largo, FL 33037

Atlantic Bay Resort
160 Sterling Rd, Tavernier, FL 33070

Coconut Palm Inn
198 Harborview Dr, Tavernier, FL 33070

Ragged Edge Resort and Marina
243 Treasure Harbor Dr, Islamorada, FL 33036

Chesapeake Beach Resort
83409 Overseas Hwy, Islamorada, FL 33036

Casa Morada
136 Madeira Rd, Islamorada, FL 33036

Islander Resort
82100 Overseas Hwy, Islamorada, FL 33036

Cheeca Lodge & Spa
81801 Overseas Hwy, Islamorada, FL 33036

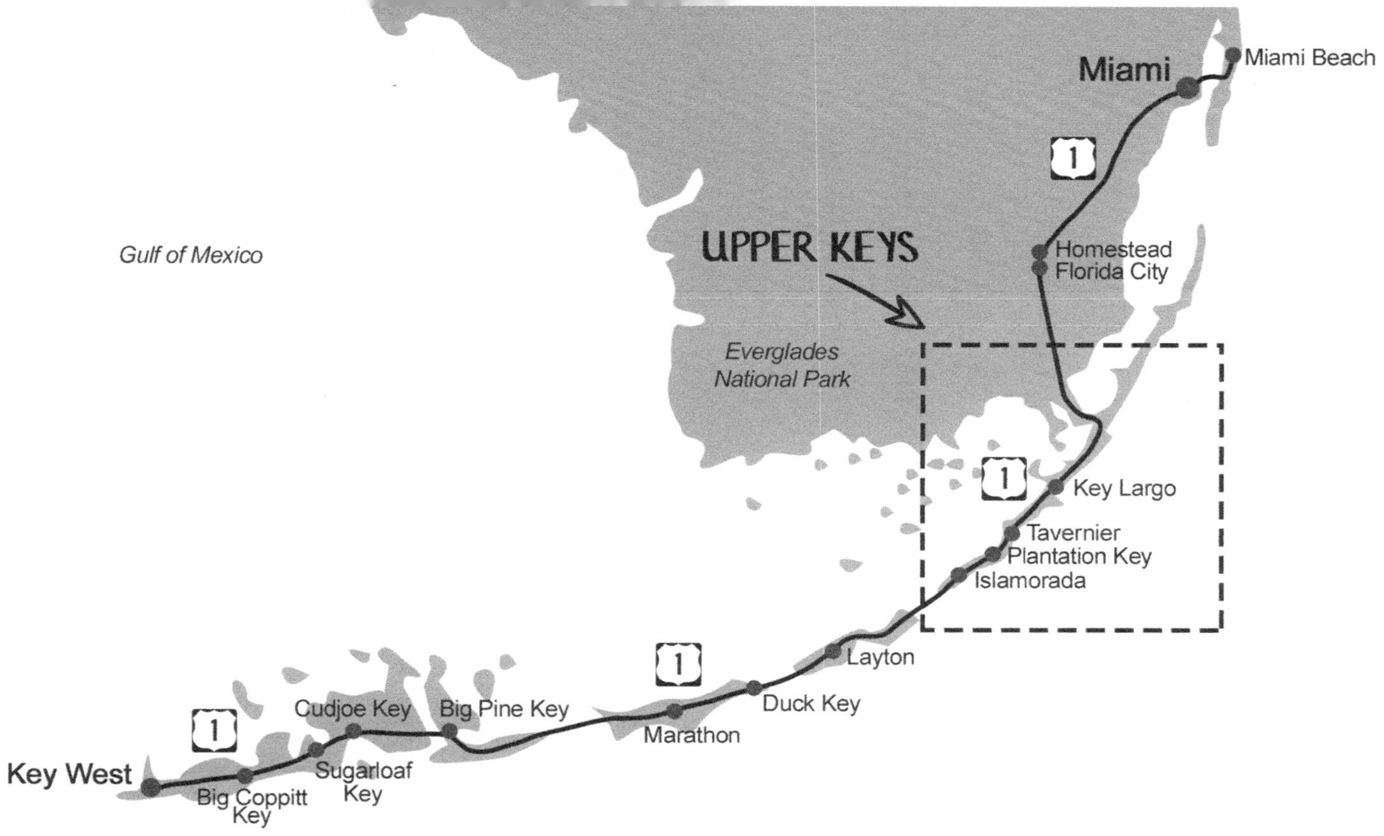

PLACES TO VISIT IN
UPPER KEYS:

(19) Overseas Highway

(20) The Florida Keys Visitor Center

(21) Key Largo Visitor Center

(22) Rowell's Waterfront Park

(23) Caribbean Club

(24) Florida Bay Outfitters

(25) Sundowners

(26) Pirates Cove Watersports

(27) John Pennekamp Coral Reef State Park

(28) Cannon Beach

(29) The Fish House

(30) Dolphins Plus Bayside

(31) Mrs. Mac's Kitchen

(32) Coco Plum Place

(33) Wild Bird Sanctuary

(34) Blond Giraffe

(35) What The Fish? Rolls & More

(36) Toilet Seat Cut

(37) Old Road Gallery

(38) Marker 88

(39) Islamorada Visitor Center

(40) Rain Barrel Village

(41) Theater of the Sea

(42) History of Diving Museum

(43) Keys History & Discovery Center

(44) Hurricane Monument

(45) Florida Keys Brewing Co

(46) Bass Pro Shops - World Wide Sportsman

(47) Lazy Days

(48) Robbie's of Islamorada

(49) Alligator Reef Lighthouse

(50) Anne's Beach

(51) Highway Piers Historical Marker

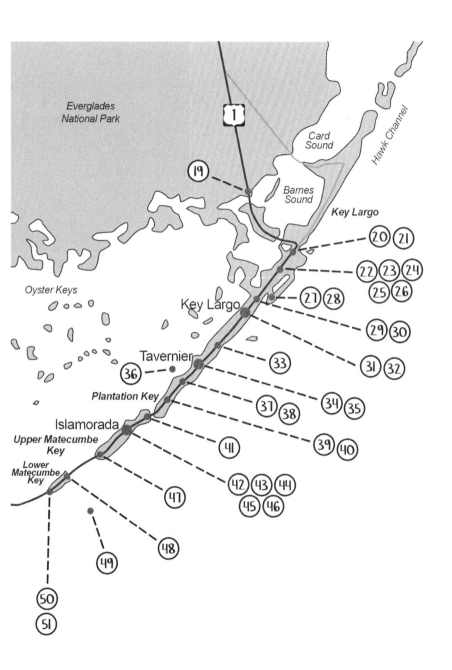

19

ICONIC PLACE

TOURIST ATTRACTION

1
OVERSEAS HIGHWAY

OVERSEAS HIGHWAY

MILEAGE: 65 MI/ 105 KM KEY LARGO, FL
OVERSEAS HIGHWAY MILE MARKER: 113 MI
25.18469, -80.38831

You are now embarking on a picturesque a 113-mile-long stretch that will lead you to the enchanting destination of Key West while traversing the exquisite Florida Keys. As you drive, you'll be captivated by breathtaking views of the Gulf of Mexico's turquoise waters on one side and the Atlantic Ocean on the other. Along this magnificent highway, you'll encounter a series of markers that commence at the 113-mile point and gradually decrease as you make your way to the ultimate destination of Key West. I incorporated the mile marker values from the Overseas Highway at subsequent points to help track your location. The beginning of the Florida Keys starts at the majestic Jewfish Creek Bridge. The bridge is 65 feet tall and opened in 2008, replacing a small drawbridge. Notably, the bridge's side and median barriers are adorned in a vivid shade known as "Belize Blue," a color thoughtfully recommended by the esteemed marine artist Robert Wyland.

Jewfish Creek Bridge
107800 Overseas Hwy, Key Largo, FL 33037

**SCAN QR CODE
TO NAVIGATE**

20

THE FLORIDA KEYS VISITOR CENTER

MILEAGE: 67 MI/ 108 KM KEY LARGO, FL
OVERSEAS HIGHWAY MILE MARKER: 106 MI
25.16950, -80.37642

Welcome to the Florida Keys! Your journey begins at the Florida Keys Visitor Center, the perfect introduction to your visit. Here, you'll receive a complimentary map, exclusive discount cards, and the opportunity to seamlessly book unforgettable tours throughout the enchanting Florida Keys. At the front of the building, you'll find two vibrant, oversized chairs, inviting countless visitors to capture memorable photos. Why not join in and create your own special moment?

The Florida Keys Visitor Center
106240 Overseas Hwy, Key Largo, FL 33037

**SCAN QR CODE
TO NAVIGATE**

KEY LARGO VISITOR CENTER

MILEAGE: 67 MI/ 108 KM KEY LARGO, FL
OVERSEAS HIGHWAY MILE MARKER: 106 MI
25.18469, -80.38831

Perhaps you're wondering why there's another visitor center so close to the previous one. The initial one focused broadly on the Florida Keys region. However, this one is centered specifically on one of the largest keys, namely Key Largo. Key Largo is a tropical paradise renowned for its unique blend of natural beauty and vibrant marine life. Nestled between the expanse of the Atlantic Ocean and the Florida Bay, this picturesque island offers a laid-back atmosphere and a range of outdoor activities. Key Largo got its name from the Spanish term "cayo largo," meaning long key. However, some historical records suggest that the name might also have originated from the abundance of human bones discovered on the island by early Spanish explorers. At the visitor center, you can discover detailed information about local events, available hotels, exciting trips, and acquire a handy map to enhance your exploration experience.

Florida Keys Visitor Center - Key Largo Chamber of Commerce
106000 Overseas Hwy, Key Largo, FL 33037

**SCAN QR CODE
TO NAVIGATE**

22

TOURIST ATTRACTION

ROWELL'S WATERFRONT PARK

MILEAGE: 69 MI/ 111 KM KEY LARGO, FL
OVERSEAS HIGHWAY MILE MARKER: 104 MI
25.15017, -80.39232

Discover an enchanting oasis at Rowell's Waterfront Park. Nestled amidst the tranquil surroundings is a deep basin perfect for snorkeling and diving enthusiasts. The quaint beach adorned with soft sands invites you to unwind and enjoy a leisurely picnic at the available tables. As the day gracefully transitions into evening, the park's vantage point becomes a captivating stage for breathtaking sunsets. Rowell's Waterfront Park is not just a destination; it's a picturesque retreat where nature's beauty unfolds in every ripple and sunset glow. Adding to its allure, Rowell's Waterfront Park is a dog-friendly haven! So, fear not and bring your furry companion along for the adventure!

Rowell's Waterfront Park
104550 Overseas Hwy, Key Largo, FL 33037

**SCAN QR CODE
TO NAVIGATE**

23

ICONIC PLACE

RESTAURANT

1
OVERSEAS HIGHWAY

CARIBBEAN CLUB

MILEAGE: 69 MI/ 111 KM KEY LARGO, FL
OVERSEAS HIGHWAY MILE MARKER: 104 MI
25.14508, -80.39686

Built in 1938 by the renowned entrepreneur Carl Fisher, the Caribbean Club stands as the oldest bar in the Upper Keys. Originally a modest fishing retreat with a hotel and restaurant, it delved into the world of gambling after Fisher's death in 1939. The iconic establishment gained Hollywood fame when Warner Brothers drew inspiration from it for the 1947 film "Key Largo," starring Humphrey Bogart and Lauren Bacall. The Caribbean Club even served as a filming location for the Netflix series "Bloodline." Purchased by the Krone family in 1948, the bar faced adversity with a suspicious fire in 1955 that destroyed the hotel. Ruth and Lefty Whitehurst took over in 1963, only to see the club damaged again in 1971 due to arson during an attempted burglary. Today, the Caribbean Club is a family affair, currently managed by Ruth and Lefty's descendants.

Caribbean Club
104080 Overseas Hwy, Key Largo, FL 33037

**SCAN QR CODE
TO NAVIGATE**

24

TOURIST ATTRACTION

1

OVERSEAS HIGHWAY

FLORIDA BAY OUTFITTERS

MILEAGE: 69 MI/ 111 KM KEY LARGO, FL
OVERSEAS HIGHWAY MILE MARKER: 104 MI
25.14454, -80.39707

Established in 1990, Florida Bay Outfitters stands as a premier paddle sport center, offering an extensive range of paddle sports equipment, mangrove tunnel tours, and top-notch kayak and paddle board rentals. Their remarkable shop is a must-visit, boasting the world's largest collection of Florida Bay Clothing. From stylish shirts and cozy sweaters to fashionable bathing suits and magically quick-drying shorts, their diverse offerings have something for everyone. This unparalleled selection ensures you'll find the perfect piece to complement your style and capture the essence of the Florida Bay experience. For an unforgettable adventure, I highly recommend indulging in the Mangrove Tunnel Kayak Adventure, a three-hour journey curated for those seeking both excitement and education. Guided by experts, participants navigate crystal-clear waters, immersing themselves in the mangroves' intricate ecosystem.

Florida Bay Outfitters - Kayaks & Clothing
104050 Overseas Hwy, Key Largo, FL 33037

**SCAN QR CODE
TO NAVIGATE**

25

SUNDOWNERS

MILEAGE: 69 MI/ 111 KM KEY LARGO, FL
OVERSEAS HIGHWAY MILE MARKER: 103 MI
25.14421, -80.39851

The fantastic Sundowners restaurant has become my go-to for delectable meals in the beautiful setting of Florida Keys. Since its inception in 1985, Sundowners in Key Largo has consistently delighted people with an enticing menu featuring a variety of sandwiches, steaks, and seafood, all served against the stunning backdrop of Florida Bay. Immerse yourself in panoramic views within the glass-walled dining room, that capture the essence of the locale. For an even more delightful experience, opt for an alfresco setting on the covered deck or tropical patio, both situated right on the shores of Florida Bay. Sundowners is particularly renowned for spectacular sunset views overlooking the Gulf of Mexico, creating a picturesque setting and an unforgettable dining experience. The combination of great food, breathtaking views, and a touch of adventure at the back dock make it an ideal destination for locals and visitors alike.

Sundowners
103900 Overseas Hwy, Key Largo, FL 33037

**SCAN QR CODE
TO NAVIGATE**

26

TOURIST ATTRACTION

1
OVERSEAS HIGHWAY

PIRATES COVE WATERSPORTS

MILEAGE: 69 MI/ 111 KM KEY LARGO, FL
OVERSEAS HIGHWAY MILE MARKER: 103 MI
25.14141, -80.40037

Prior to venturing further into the enchanting waters of the Florida Keys, ensure you're well-prepared for underwater adventures. Fun Fact: The Upper Keys you are currently traveling through are island remnants of ancient coral reefs. Don't overlook the importance of having proper diving equipment! If, by any chance, you find yourself without even the most basic snorkeling mask, consider making a swift stop at Pirates Cove Watersports. You'll find a comprehensive selection of diving gear there. This shop is an essential hub for those who are passionate about exploring the underwater world, offering a wide range of products and services to support novice and experienced divers. This includes items such as wetsuits, masks, fins, regulators, tanks, and other essential gear. Knowledgeable staff will assist you in selecting the right equipment based on your individual needs, preferences, and skill levels. At Pirates Cove Watersports, you can also purchase diving or snorkeling trips with experienced instructors, as well as scuba diving lessons.

Pirates Cove Watersports
103800 Overseas Hwy, Key Largo, FL 33037

**SCAN QR CODE
TO NAVIGATE**

TO VISIT
VISITED

27

 ICONIC PLACE

 NATURAL LANDMARK

 1 OVERSEAS HIGHWAY

JOHN PENNEKAMP
CORAL REEF STATE PARK

MILEAGE: 71 MI/ 114 KM KEY LARGO, FL
OVERSEAS HIGHWAY MILE MARKER: 102 MI
25.12517, -80.40612

Welcome to John Pennekamp Coral Reef State Park, a tropical paradise nestled in the heart of the Florida Keys. Known as the first undersea park in the United States, this aquatic wonderland offers a captivating blend of vibrant coral reefs, crystal-clear waters, and diverse marine life. Named after the famed conservationist John D. Pennekamp, the park spans over 70 nautical square miles, making it a haven for snorkelers, divers, and nature enthusiasts. For those who prefer to stay dry, glass-bottom boat tours provide a window into the marine world below, offering a unique perspective without getting wet. Beyond its aquatic wonders, John Pennekamp Coral Reef State Park offers hiking trails, picnic areas, and a visitor center with informative exhibits on the park's rich natural history.

Visitor Center and Aquarium
102601 Overseas Hwy, Key Largo, FL 33037

**SCAN QR CODE
TO NAVIGATE**

☐ TO VISIT
☐ VISITED

28

NATURAL LANDMARK

1 OVERSEAS HIGHWAY

CANNON BEACH

MILEAGE: 71 MI/ 114 KM KEY LARGO, FL
OVERSEAS HIGHWAY MILE MARKER: 102 MI
25.12574, -80.40545

Just a stone's throw away from the park visitor center we explored in the previous point, Cannon Beach emerges as an enticing choice for your Florida Keys inaugural beach experience. Nestled in Key Largo, this beach is a highly sought-after destination for shoreline snorkeling enthusiasts. Situated within the confines of the John Pennekamp Coral Reef State Park, it boasts a unique attraction—an ancient Spanish shipwreck adorned with its original anchor and cannons, now embraced by a vibrant array of marine life. Ever wondered about the origins of its name? Even if this is your maiden voyage to Cannon Beach, you'll swiftly unravel the historical tale behind one of the two pristine beaches within the park. Along the sun-kissed expanse of Cannon Beach lies a collection of authentic 17th-century cannons, proudly standing as silent witnesses to Florida's rich and storied past. It's not just a beach; it's a captivating journey through time.

Cannon Beach
102601 Overseas Hwy, Key Largo, FL 33037

**SCAN QR CODE
TO NAVIGATE**

THE FISH HOUSE

MILEAGE: 71 MI/ 114 KM KEY LARGO, FL
OVERSEAS HIGHWAY MILE MARKER: 102 MI
25.12428, -80.41295

The Fish House Restaurant and Seafood Market is a charming and iconic establishment that has become synonymous with the Florida Keys' laid-back, coastal lifestyle. Situated in the heart of Key Largo, the Fish House offers a unique blend of fresh seafood, vibrant atmosphere, and a touch of local charm. It is one of the few remaining establishments that only buys whole fish from local commercial fishermen, and a few other select vendors. Stone Crab and Lobster, when in season, are also brought fresh off the boat by local trappers. This place has garnered widespread recognition, making notable appearances on popular television programs like 'Diners, Drive-Ins, and Dives,' 'Man v. Food,' and various other shows. Absolutely a fantastic choice for enjoying fresh fish and seafood when you find yourself in the Florida Keys!

The Fish House
102401 Overseas Hwy, Key Largo, FL 33037

**SCAN QR CODE
TO NAVIGATE**

30

TOURIST
ATTRACTION

1

OVERSEAS
HIGHWAY

DOLPHINS PLUS BAYSIDE

MILEAGE: 72 MI/ 116 KM KEY LARGO, FL
OVERSEAS HIGHWAY MILE MARKER: 101 MI

25.11902, -80.41905

Dolphins Plus Bayside is known for its focus on education, research, and the conservation of marine mammals, particularly dolphins. This place features various interactive programs that allow visitors to get up close and personal with dolphins. These programs include swimming with dolphins, dolphin encounters, and trainer for a day experiences. Participants have the chance to touch, play, and even swim alongside these incredible animals under the guidance of experienced trainers. The facility also emphasizes education about marine life and the importance of conservation. Through guided tours, presentations, and informational sessions, visitors can gain insights into the behavior, communication, and ecological significance of dolphins. The goal is to raise awareness about the challenges facing marine environments and the need for conservation efforts.

Dolphins Plus Bayside
101900 Overseas Hwy, Key Largo, FL 33037

**SCAN QR CODE
TO NAVIGATE**

TO VISIT
VISITED

31

MRS. MAC'S KITCHEN

MILEAGE: 74 MI/ 119 KM KEY LARGO, FL
OVERSEAS HIGHWAY MILE MARKER: 99 MI
25.09203, -80.44396

This stop is a well-known eating spot popular among locals and visitors along the Overseas Highway. Discover the timeless charm of Mrs. Mac's Kitchen, a beloved establishment in the heart of the Florida Keys. Founded in 1976 by Jeff Macfarland and named after his mother, Mrs. Mac's embodies the rustic allure of the old Keys, where time slows down and community spirit thrives. Renowned for an extensive menu catering to diverse palates, Mrs. Mac's is a local treasure, celebrated for its iconic Key lime pie. With two convenient highway locations, this is more than a pit stop, it's a community hub where shared stories and delicious dishes come together. What truly sets Mrs. Mac's apart is not just its culinary prowess but its exceptional staff. Committed, expert, and customer-centric, they are the backbone of the restaurant. Under caring ownership, the legacy continues with the enduring motto: "Eat well, laugh often, live long."

Mrs. Mac's Kitchen (Little)
99336 Overseas Hwy, Key Largo, FL 33037

**SCAN QR CODE
TO NAVIGATE**

32

COCO PLUM PLACE

MILEAGE: 75 MI/ 121 KM KEY LARGO, FL
OVERSEAS HIGHWAY MILE MARKER: 98 MI
25.08093, -80.45472

Now, it's time for a coffee break! If you're searching for a serene spot to enjoy your favorite coffee, consider visiting Coco Plum Place. It's an incredibly relaxed and tranquil cafe, complete with charming outdoor garden seating areas—a true hidden oasis. This is the perfect spot for a leisurely breakfast or lunch. Their menu provides plenty of vegan options too. From bowls and smoothies to wraps and toasts, there's something for everyone. If you're looking for healthy food, look no further. The cafe is not only aesthetically pleasing but also houses a shop with a diverse range of items, from candles to postcards.

Coco Plum Place
98275 Overseas Hwy, Key Largo, FL 33037

**SCAN QR CODE
TO NAVIGATE**

WILD BIRD SANCTUARY

MILEAGE: 79 MI/ 127 KM TAVERNIER, FL
OVERSEAS HIGHWAY MILE MARKER: 93 MI
25.03195, -80.50396

The Florida Keys Wild Bird Center stands as a testament to the dedication of wildlife conservationists and serves as a haven for avian inhabitants in the picturesque Florida Keys. Established with a mission to rescue, rehabilitate, and release injured birds, this center has evolved into a vital sanctuary. The sanctuary spans several acres, providing a natural environment where injured, sick, or orphaned birds can receive expert care. The center is not only a refuge for these feathered creatures but also a hub for education and awareness about the importance of preserving bird habitats. One of the key attractions of the Florida Keys Wild Bird Center is the extensive range of bird species that call the sanctuary home, from majestic herons and egrets to colorful parrots and pelicans. Visitors can observe the birds in spacious aviaries that mimic their natural habitats, allowing for a more authentic experience.

Florida Keys Wild Bird Center - Bird Sanctuary
93600 Overseas Hwy, Tavernier, FL 33070

**SCAN QR CODE
TO NAVIGATE**

☐ TO VISIT
☐ VISITED

34

BLOND GIRAFFE

MILEAGE: 81 MI/ 130 KM TAVERNIER, FL
OVERSEAS HIGHWAY MILE MARKER: 92 MI
25.01318, -80.51377

Renowned among travelers and visitors alike, this establishment has garnered attention on various TV shows such as Food Finds on the Food Network, Unwrapped on the Food Network, and Food Wars on the Travel Channel, in addition to numerous awards. Famous for serving the finest pies in the Florida Keys, the Blond Giraffe invites you to savor their award-winning key lime pie in the serene ambiance of their garden. Take a respite from the hustle and bustle of your busy day as you enjoy a slice of delectable pie paired with a cup of coffee or a refreshing key-limeade. Don't miss the opportunity to commemorate your love by placing a lock on their Love Lock Way with those nearest to your heart. Capture the beauty of the moment with a stunning photo against the backdrop of their mural, artfully painted by Shoker Art 1. Treat yourself to this delightful and charming slice of heaven – a must-visit destination!

Blond Giraffe Key Lime Pie Factory
92220 Overseas Hwy, Tavernier, FL 33070

**SCAN QR CODE
TO NAVIGATE**

RESTAURANT

1

OVERSEAS HIGHWAY

WHAT THE FISH? ROLLS & MORE

MILEAGE: 82 MI/ 132 KM TAVERNIER, FL
OVERSEAS HIGHWAY MILE MARKER: 90 MI
25.00229, -80.53159

This place is an another must-stop for foodies! Make a visit to What The Fish? Rolls & More for the best rolls and tacos based on locally caught seafood. A personal favorite of mine is the delectable Roller Lobster, a roll that epitomizes the perfect fusion of succulent lobster and tantalizing flavors. Additionally, the Shrimp Taco is a culinary masterpiece, showcasing the delicate taste of impeccably prepared shrimp. They provide an excellent array of beverages and feature an outdoor patio, where guests can enjoy the delightful water-canal vibe.

What The Fish? Rolls & More
90775 Old Hwy Unit #6, Tavernier, FL 33070

**SCAN QR CODE
TO NAVIGATE**

36

TOILET SEAT CUT

MILEAGE: 83 MI/ 134 KM TAVERNIER, FL
OVERSEAS HIGHWAY MILE MARKER: 90 MI
24.99854, -80.55181

Situated near mile marker 90 in the picturesque locale of Islamorada, The Toilet Seat Cut, a genuine tourist hotspot, can be found amidst the tranquil waters of Florida Bay. About 250 decorated toilet seats line a 60-foot-wide manmade channel near mangrove islands and seagrass flats. A five-foot-tall pirate and mailbox are part of the decorations planted in the marl as well. This quirky installation not only serves as a unique visual experience but also facilitates boat travel, connecting the western expanse of Plantation Key to its eastern counterpart. Toilet Seat Cut, a man-made channel in the Florida Keys, was dredged by local resident Vernon Lamp in the mid-20th century for a quicker route to Plantation Yacht Club. Evading strict sea grass laws, Lamp marked the passage with homemade posts. Hurricane Donna in 1960 scattered debris, including a toilet seat on a marker. Locals embraced the humor, decorating other posts with toilet seats for various occasions. If you would like to go there, you can, for example, rent a jet ski at JSK Watersports located near Tavernier.

Toilet Seat Cut
24.99854, -80.55181

**SCAN QR CODE
TO NAVIGATE**

OLD ROAD GALLERY

MILEAGE: 84 MI/ 135 KM TAVERNIER, FL
OVERSEAS HIGHWAY MILE MARKER: 88 MI
25.03195, -80.50396

While exploring new destinations, I make it a point to support local artists. If you share a passion for the arts, don't miss the chance to discover the enchanting Old Road Gallery, a hidden gem worth exploring. Established in 2014, The Old Road Gallery, situated between US 1 and the Old Road, is a haven created by owners and artists Dwayne and Cindy King. With two decades of experience behind them, the couple initially crafted, exhibited, and sold unique bronze, copper, and clay masterpieces at their first venue, Rain Barrel Sculpture Gallery. Now situated at mile marker 88.8, their new property and gallery unfolds as a secluded sanctuary, surrounded by native hardwoods and meandering pathways. During your visit, take a moment to explore the outdoor attractions, including the operational pottery studio, copper workshop, and the serene Sculpture Garden.

Old Road Gallery
88888 Old Hwy, Tavernier, FL 33070

**SCAN QR CODE
TO NAVIGATE**

TO VISIT

VISITED

38

MARKER 88

MILEAGE: 85 MI/ 137 KM ISLAMORADA, FL
OVERSEAS HIGHWAY MILE MARKER: 88 MI
24.97146, -80.55776

You are now approaching Mile Marker 88 on the Overseas Highway, where the restaurant of the same name is located. Immerse yourself in the laid-back ambiance as you peruse a menu brimming with the bounty of the sea. From succulent seafood to hand-crafted cocktails and locally brewed beverages, Marker 88 promises a gastronomic journey through the essence of Florida's coastal cuisine. Discover the allure of dining with your toes in the sand at their beachside tables. Furthermore, Marker 88 isn't just a culinary destination; it's a shopping haven. Explore the gift shops at Marker 88, where you can find unique treasures to commemorate your coastal experience. Whether you're a seafood enthusiast, a cocktail aficionado, or simply seeking a taste of the local brew, savor the essence of the Sunshine State at this mile marker oasis.

Marker 88
88000 Overseas Hwy, Islamorada, FL 33036

**SCAN QR CODE
TO NAVIGATE**

39

ISLAMORADA VISITOR CENTER

MILEAGE: 86 MI/ 138 KM ISLAMORADA, FL
OVERSEAS HIGHWAY MILE MARKER: 87 MI
24.96065, -80.56792

Welcome to Islamorada, a picturesque paradise nestled in the Florida Keys, beckoning visitors with an enchanting blend of sun-kissed beaches, crystal-clear waters, and a vibrant marine ecosystem. Known as the "Purple Island," the name harkens back to the days of Spanish exploration when the region's beauty left a lasting impression. Islamorada rests along migration routes for many large fish species, earning it the informal title of "Sportfishing Capital of the World." This tropical haven comprises a chain of islands, each contributing to the area's unique charm. From world-class fishing and water sports to serene sunsets that paint the sky with hues of purple and gold, Islamorada is ideal for nature enthusiasts and leisure seekers alike. To begin exploring, I recommend visiting the Islamorada Chamber of Commerce & Visitors Center. There, you can obtain information about current events and acquire a map of the area.
Additionally, they have a small gift shop.

Islamorada Chamber Of Commerce & Visitors Center
87100 Overseas Hwy, Islamorada, FL 33036

**SCAN QR CODE
TO NAVIGATE**

40

ICONIC
PLACE

TOURIST
ATTRACTION

1

OVERSEAS
HIGHWAY

RAIN BARREL VILLAGE

MILEAGE: 87 MI/ 140 KM ISLAMORADA, FL
OVERSEAS HIGHWAY MILE MARKER: 86 MI
24.95932, -80.57124

The first thing people notice about Rain Barrel Village is Betsy the Lobster. This colossal sculpture looms large over the gateway to this unique property. With its impressive 30-foot height and sprawling 40-foot length, Betsy is not merely a striking sight but also a symbolic representation of the diverse wildlife found in the Keys. This colossal Spiny Lobster has become a beloved landmark just off the Overseas Highway, captivating visitors who flock to capture an unforgettable photo opportunity. Renowned for its charm, Rain Barrel Village consistently earns acclaim in both national and local publications as a premier destination. Wander through picturesque gardens along shaded pathways and explore their intimate studios showcasing an array of meticulously crafted items. From contemporary artwork and handmade crafts to beachwear, home goods, and unique Florida Keys-inspired souvenirs, there's something for everyone. Are you ready to take a selfie with Betsy the Lobster?

Rain Barrel Village
88000 Overseas Hwy, Islamorada, FL 33036

**SCAN QR CODE
TO NAVIGATE**

TO VISIT
VISITED

41

THEATER OF THE SEA

MILEAGE: 89 MI/ 143 KM ISLAMORADA, FL
OVERSEAS HIGHWAY MILE MARKER: 84 MI

24.94442, -80.60386

Theater of the Sea, located in Islamorada, is a unique and captivating marine mammal park that stands out as one of the most popular attractions in this picturesque Florida Keys destination. Founded in 1946, Theater of the Sea has a rich history and has been a pioneer in providing interactive marine experiences. The park is home to a diverse array of marine animals, including dolphins, sea lions, sea turtles, and various species of fish and birds. The primary mission of the facility extends beyond entertainment, emphasizing education and fostering an appreciation for marine life and conservation. One of the key highlights of Theater of the Sea is its engaging and informative live shows featuring trained dolphins and sea lions. These performances not only entertain audiences but also educate them about the intelligence, agility, and social behaviors of these incredible marine mammals. Visitors have the opportunity to witness awe-inspiring demonstrations showcasing the strong bond between the animals and their trainers.

Theater of the Sea
84721 Overseas Hwy, Islamorada, FL 33036

**SCAN QR CODE
TO NAVIGATE**

42

ICONIC PLACE

MUSEUM

1
OVERSEAS HIGHWAY

HISTORY OF DIVING MUSEUM

MILEAGE: 90 MI/ 145 KM ISLAMORADA, FL
OVERSEAS HIGHWAY MILE MARKER: 82 MI
24.93112, -80.62079

The first thing people notice about Rain Barrel Village is Betsy the Lobster. This colossal sculpture looms large over the gateway to this unique property. With its impressive 30-foot height and sprawling 40-foot length, Betsy is not merely a striking sight but also a symbolic representation of the diverse wildlife found in the Keys. This colossal Spiny Lobster has become a beloved landmark just off the Overseas Highway, captivating visitors who flock to capture an unforgettable photo opportunity. Renowned for its charm, Rain Barrel Village consistently earns acclaim in both national and local publications as a premier destination. Wander through picturesque gardens along shaded pathways and explore their intimate studios showcasing an array of meticulously crafted items. From contemporary artwork and handmade crafts to beachwear, home goods, and unique Florida Keys-inspired souvenirs, there's something for everyone. Are you ready to take a selfie with Betsy the Lobster?

History of Diving Museum
82990 Overseas Hwy, Islamorada, FL 33036

**SCAN QR CODE
TO NAVIGATE**

TO VISIT
VISITED

43

MUSEUM

1
OVERSEAS
HIGHWAY

KEYS HISTORY & DISCOVERY CENTER

MILEAGE: 91 MI/ 146 KM ISLAMORADA, FL
OVERSEAS HIGHWAY MILE MARKER: 82 MI
24.92097, -80.62947

Another interesting museum worth visiting in Islamorada is the Keys History & Discovery Center. Explore exhibits like First People, Native Americans, Pirates, Wreckers, Salvagers, and Spanish Treasure Fleets. Dive into the legends of the Upper Keys, from Henry Flagler's Over-Sea Railway to the challenges faced by the unique coral reef ecosystem. The museum showcases a 16th-century cannon and an 18th-century anchor from shipwrecks, highlighting the area's maritime past. Don't miss the Coral Reef Exploration exhibit in partnership with Mote Marine Laboratory. The second floor features a rotating exhibit space, the Jerry Wilkinson Research Library, and a 35-seat theater with documentaries on local history. Experience the vibrant stories of Islamorada's past in this fascinating museum.

Keys History & Discovery Center
82100 Overseas Hwy, Islamorada, FL 33036

**SCAN QR CODE
TO NAVIGATE**

44

HISTORICAL LANDMARK

1

OVERSEAS HIGHWAY

HURRICANE MONUMENT

MILEAGE: 92 MI/ 148 KM ISLAMORADA, FL
OVERSEAS HIGHWAY MILE MARKER: 81 MI
24.91709, -80.63592

As you bask in the warm embrace of the Florida Keys sunshine while cruising along the Overseas Highway, there's a subtle reminder tucked away in Islamorada that may not immediately capture your attention. Amidst the breathtaking views on either side, the unassuming Hurricane Monument quietly stands, a piece of history that you may have unintentionally passed. Crafted from the native coral limestone, this seemingly modest memorial marks the profound significance of the 1935 Hurricane. Its unpretentious appearance might not immediately convey the depth of its meaning, and many travelers inadvertently overlook it. Yet, for the resilient residents of the Florida Keys, this humble structure speaks volumes, preserving the memory of a momentous event in the region's history. So, as you journey through the scenic Overseas Highway, consider a brief pause to explore the Hurricane Monument—a simple yet poignant tribute to the enduring spirit of this coastal community.

Hurricane Monument
81831 Old Hwy, Islamorada, FL 33036

**SCAN QR CODE
TO NAVIGATE**

45

FLORIDA KEYS BREWING CO

MILEAGE: 92 MI/ 148 KM ISLAMORADA, FL
OVERSEAS HIGHWAY MILE MARKER: 81 MI
24.91556, -80.63758

Florida Keys Brewing Company is the Upper Keys' first microbrewery, offering a diverse selection of both crowd favorites and a rotating list of seasonal and barrel-aged beers on draft. Established in 2014 by Craig McBay and his wife Cheryl, the brewery emerged from their desire to blend their love of fishing with a passion for brewing beer. Utilizing various-sized fermentation tanks, including small ones for crafting specialty beers, the company produces its own unique brews. What distinguishes Florida Keys Brewing Company is its unwavering commitment to providing patrons with an authentic taste of Florida through locally crafted products. With a rich history, the brewery has become synonymous with some of Florida's most beloved beers.

Florida Keys Brewing Co
81611 Old Hwy, Islamorada, FL 33036

**SCAN QR CODE
TO NAVIGATE**

46

WORLD WIDE SPORTSMAN

MILEAGE: 92 MI/ 148 KM ISLAMORADA, FL
OVERSEAS HIGHWAY MILE MARKER: 81 MI
24.91481, -80.63972

Calling all souvenir enthusiasts and adventure seekers! A must-stop destination for your Florida Keys expedition is the iconic World Wide Sportsman—a sprawling emporium where the thrill of sportsmanship meets the charm of souvenir hunting. Not only a haven for those in search of memorabilia to commemorate their journey, World Wide Sportsman also boasts an extensive collection of sports and fishing equipment. As you explore the store's offerings, a captivating surprise awaits: the Hemingway Pilar. This detailed reproduction of Ernest Hemingway's cherished fishing vessel adds an extra layer of allure to your shopping experience. However, it's essential to note that this isn't the same Pilar acquired by Hemingway in 1934 after his African safari. The authentic Pilar is a historic treasure now displayed at the Museo Ernest Hemingway in Cuba, under the care of the Cuban government. In its place, World Wide Sportsman proudly showcases the sister ship, sharing the same iconic name.

Bass Pro Shops - World Wide Sportsman
81576 Overseas Hwy, Islamorada, FL 33036

**SCAN QR CODE
TO NAVIGATE**

47

LAZY DAYS

MILEAGE: 93 MI/ 150 KM ISLAMORADA, FL
OVERSEAS HIGHWAY MILE MARKER: 79 MI
24.89828, -80.65703

Lazy Days is a highly acclaimed and popular restaurant located in Islamorada. Indulge in a serene oceanfront dining experience while savoring delectable Keys-style dishes. The menu at Lazy Days features a variety of options, including fresh seafood, seafood pastas, vegetarian pastas, sandwiches, and certified Angus steaks to be enjoyed in a wide range of surroundings. First of all, there's beach dining—a casual experience with spectacular views from tables nestled in the sand. The second option is patio dining, where you can enjoy your meal on their outside upstairs patio overlooking the beautiful waters of the Atlantic. Another choice is porch dining—an interior side porch with sliding glass doors framing beautiful ocean views. The last option is the cozy interior within the restaurant. After enjoying your meal, relax on their beach and soak up the sun with a drink in hand!

Lazy Days Restaurant
79867 Overseas Hwy, Islamorada, FL 33036

**SCAN QR CODE
TO NAVIGATE**

48

ICONIC PLACE

TOURIST ATTRACTION

1
OVERSEAS HIGHWAY

ROBBIE'S OF ISLAMORADA
MILEAGE: 96 MI/ 154 KM ISLAMORADA, FL
OVERSEAS HIGHWAY MILE MARKER: 77 MI
24.88259, -80.69079

Absolutely, a must-stop during your Overseas Highway journey is the famous and iconic Robbie's of Islamorada, home of the world-famous tarpon feeding! Robbie and his wife, Mona, began feeding Scarface 18 years ago after rescuing the injured tarpon. With stitches from Doc Roach to repair his torn jaw, Scarface recovered and became part of Robbie's history. Now voted the top destination in The Keys, Robbie's offers handfeeding of massive tarpons, thrilling water sports, and unique souvenirs. Enjoy fresh seafood and signature cocktails at the waterfront Hungry Tarpon Restaurant. A must-visit in the Florida Keys, Robbie's Marina of Islamorada guarantees a memorable time with family and friends. It's not a trip to the Keys without a stop at Robbie's!

Robbie's of Islamorada
77522 Overseas Hwy, Islamorada, FL 33036

**SCAN QR CODE
TO NAVIGATE**

49

ALLIGATOR REEF LIGHTHOUSE

MILEAGE: 96 MI/ 154 KM ISLAMORADA, FL
OVERSEAS HIGHWAY MILE MARKER: 77 MI
24.85177, -80.61882

This historic lighthouse named Alligator Reef Lighthouse proudly stands just shy of five nautical miles off the shores of Islamorada. Accessible only by water vessel, if you're eager to explore this unique piece of history consider embarking on a boat trip from Robbie's of Islamorada. The lighthouse owes its name to the U.S. Navy schooner Alligator, a crucial member of the historic U.S. Navy Anti-Piracy Squadron in Key West. In 1822, the Alligator unfortunately ran aground at this precise location. In a strategic move to thwart potential pirate use, the vessel was deliberately exploded after salvaging valuable items. The Alligator Reef has witnessed the demise of numerous vessels on its rugged coral terrain, adding layers of maritime history to its depths. So, fret not about alligators! A mesmerizing coral reef, perfect for snorkeling enthusiasts awaits!

Alligator Reef Lighthouse
24.85177, -80.61882

**SCAN QR CODE
TO NAVIGATE**

50

ANNE'S BEACH

MILEAGE: 100 MI/ 161 KM ISLAMORADA, FL
OVERSEAS HIGHWAY MILE MARKER: 73 MI
24.84854, -80.74096

Nestled at mile marker 73.5 on the southern edge of Upper Matecumbe Key, Anne's Beach composes a unique gem in the Florida Keys—a natural sandy haven that won't cost you a dime. Comprising two parking lots and restroom facilities, the park is connected by a captivating 1,300-foot boardwalk, weaving its way through the enchanting mangroves. Lined with six pavilions boasting inviting picnic tables, this destination offers an unparalleled setting for a Keys-style picnic. But who is the eponymous Anne? The answer lies with local environmentalist Anne Eaton. Enchanted by the allure of the Keys in the 1960s, she purchased a historic house constructed from Dade County pine and fully embraced the Keys' unique way of life, eventually making it her permanent home. Anne played a pivotal role in advocating against the over-development threatening the delicate ecosystem. Her efforts extended to fundraising for the preservation of the pristine stretch of beach that now bears her name.

Anne's Beach
73500 Overseas Hwy, Islamorada, FL 33036

**SCAN QR CODE
TO NAVIGATE**

TO VISIT
VISITED

51

HIGHWAY PIERS
HISTORICAL MARKER

MILEAGE: 96 MI/ 154 KM ISLAMORADA, FL
OVERSEAS HIGHWAY MILE MARKER: 77 MI
24.84516, -80.74764

If you have an appreciation for history, make sure not to overlook this significant marker near Anne's Beach. The parking lot boasts an intriguing historical marker well worth a brief stop. This marker commemorates a pivotal moment in history related to World War I veterans. In the early 1930s, amid the Great Depression, veterans were promised a bonus but faced challenges due to a lack of government funds. President Roosevelt responded by creating the Florida Emergency Relief Administration to provide jobs. In November 1934, 600 veterans were sent to build bridges. The main camp was located where the Boy Scout Sea Base now stands. Tragically, the Labor Day hurricane on September 2, 1935, with 200 mph winds and 20-foot waves, destroyed the camp and railway. The road was later rebuilt on the railway foundations, leaving incomplete piers as a memorial to those who lost their lives in the hurricane.

Highway Piers Historical Marker
73000 Overseas Hwy, Islamorada, FL 33036

**SCAN QR CODE
TO NAVIGATE**

'IN THE FLORIDA KEYS, THE ONLY RUSH HOUR IS
WHEN THE SUN DIPS BELOW THE HORIZON,
CASTING THE WORLD IN HUES OF GOLD AND CORAL.'

UNKNOWN

WELCOME TO
MIDDLE KEYS

WHERE TO PARK YOUR RV IN MIDDLE KEYS:

This is a list of recommended RV Parks selected for a safe and comfortable stay:

RV PARKS

Fiesta Key RV Resort and Marina
70001 Overseas Hwy, Layton, FL 33001

Jolly Roger RV Resort
59275 Overseas Hwy, Marathon, FL 33050

Grassy Key RV Park & Resort
58671 Overseas Hwy, Marathon, FL 33050

Bonefish Bay Motel & RV Sites
12565 Overseas Hwy #3534, Marathon, FL 33050

Coconut Cay RV Park and Marina
7200 Aviation Blvd, Marathon, FL 33050

Ocean Breeze RV Park & Marina
1337 Ocean Breeze Ave, Marathon, FL 33050

Marathon Marina & Rv Resort
725 11th Street Ocean, Marathon, FL 33050

WHERE TO STAY IN MIDDLE KEYS:

RESORTS/HOTELS

Lime Tree Bay Resort
Mile Marker 68, FL-5, Layton, FL 33001

Conch Key Fishing Lodge & Marina
3 N Conch Ave, Conch Key, FL 33050

Hawks Cay Resort
61 Hawks Cay Blvd, Duck Key, FL 33050

Grassy Flats Resort & Beach Club
58182 Overseas Hwy, Marathon, FL 33050

Hampton Inn Marathon - Florida Keys
13351 Overseas Hwy, Marathon, FL 33050

Continental Inn
1121 W Ocean Dr, Key Colony Beach, FL 33051

Skipjack Resort & Marina
19 Sombrero Blvd, Marathon, FL 33050

Marlin Bay Resort & Marina
3800 Gulfview Ave, Marathon, FL 33050

Tranquility Bay Beachfront Resort
2600 Overseas Hwy, Marathon, FL 33050

Courtyard by Marriott Faro Blanco Resort
2146 Overseas Hwy, Marathon, FL 33050

Isla Bella Beach Resort
1 Knights Key Blvd, Marathon, FL 33050, United States

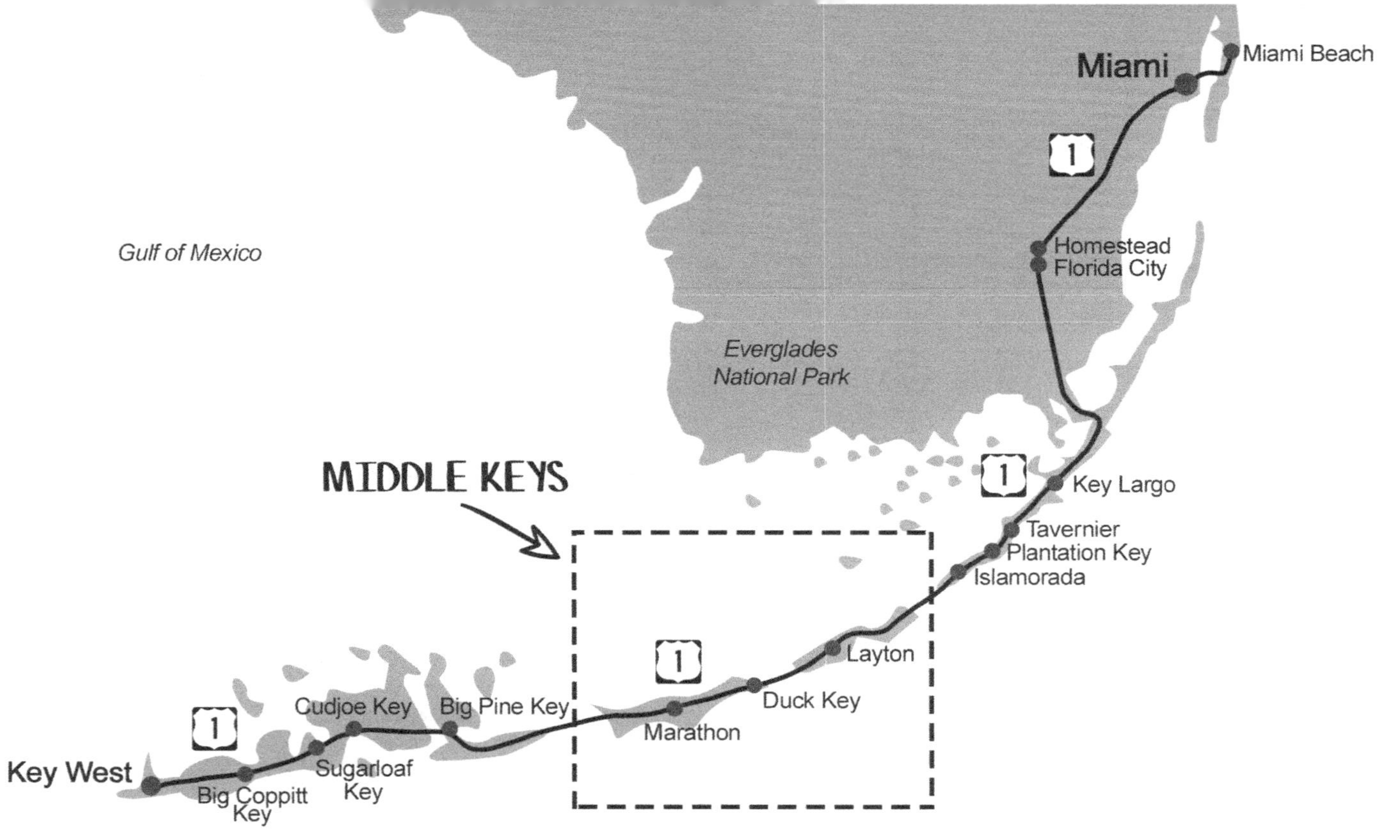

PLACES TO VISIT IN
MIDDLE KEYS:

(52) Channel #5 Bridge

(53) Oceans305

(54) Long Key Fishing Club

(55) Bongo's Botanical Beer Garden and Cafe

(56) Dolphin Research Center

(57) Sunset Park

(58) Marathon Visitor Center

(59) Florida Keys Aquarium Encounters

(60) Curly's Coffee and Marina

(61) Marathon Air Museum

(62) Florida East Coast Overseas Railroad Car

(63) Crane Point Hammock

(64) Sombrero Beach

(65) Keys Fisheries

(66) Turtle Hospital

(67) Sunset Grille & Raw Bar

(68) Seven Mile Bridge

(69) Fred the Tree

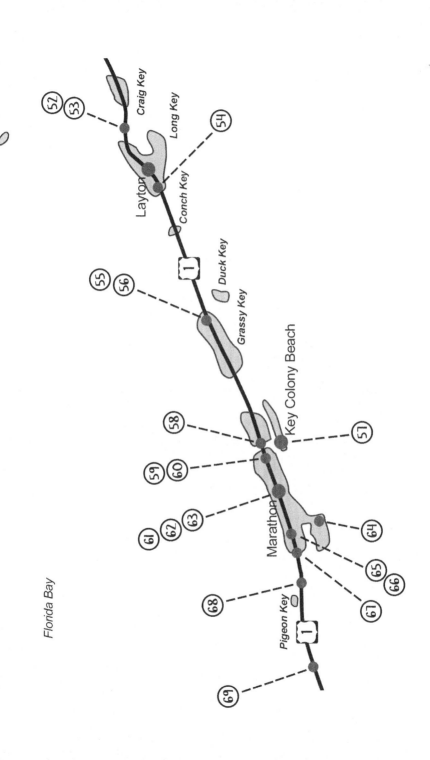

52

CHANNEL #5 BRIDGE

MILEAGE: 102 MI/ 164 KM LAYTON, FL
OVERSEAS HIGHWAY MILE MARKER: 71 MI
24.83795, -80.77313

The Channel 5 Bridge is one of the more popular bridges you will cross during your Overseas Highway journey. It offers great photo opportunities as you traverse it, with breathtaking views of the ocean on both sides. Adjacent to this bridge, you'll find the old bridge originally constructed by the Florida East Coast Railway, which was retrofitted for automobile traffic after 1935 and later closed. Today, it has been repurposed as part of the Florida Keys Overseas Heritage Trail, allowing access for both bikes and pedestrians. Towards the end of the bridge, there is a parking lot on the right where you can conveniently park your car. From there, you can take a leisurely stroll, enjoy the surroundings, or even try your hand at fishing.

Channel #5 Bridge
Florida Keys Overseas Heritage Trail, Layton, FL 33001

**SCAN QR CODE
TO NAVIGATE**

53

RESTAURANT

1

OVERSEAS
HIGHWAY

OCEANS305

MILEAGE: 103 MI/ 166 KM LAYTON, FL
OVERSEAS HIGHWAY MILE MARKER: 70 MI
24.84335, -80.79144

Oceans305 is a fantastic restaurant situated just a short distance from the Overseas Highway, providing a tranquil and relaxing atmosphere. I enjoyed taking a break here to savor the delicious food and drinks on their beach, complete with comfortable seating and umbrellas. The restaurant offers a delightful selection of appetizers, including mozzarella sticks and fried calamari, as well as excellent salads, sandwiches, and pastas. After indulging in a delightful meal, unwind on one of the sunbeds and soak up the sun. The restaurant is nestled on the beach under the shade of palm trees, creating a serene and picturesque setting for a perfect dining experience. Oceans305 truly offers a blend of delectable cuisine and a soothing beachside ambiance, making it an ideal spot to relax and enjoy a memorable meal.

Oceans305
70001 Overseas Hwy, Layton, FL 33001

**SCAN QR CODE
TO NAVIGATE**

54

LONG KEY
FISHING CLUB MARKER

MILEAGE: 108 MI/ 174 KM LAYTON, FL
OVERSEAS HIGHWAY MILE MARKER: 65 MI
24.80416, -80.84707

Another interesting spot for history buffs is the Long Key Fishing Club. A historic information panel details the story of this place, but it's challenging to spot while driving down the road. In 1906, Flagler's East Coast Hotel Company established the exclusive Long Key Fishing Club, a renowned fishing destination referred to as the "Garden of Eden." Zane Grey, the president of the Long Key Fishing Club, led efforts to conserve game fish species. The hurricane of September 2, 1935, devastated the Florida Keys, destroying the Long Key Fishing Club and ending the Key West Extension's operation. Notable figures like Herbert Hoover, Franklin Roosevelt, Andrew Mellon, and William Hearst frequented the luxurious fishing resort which featured cottages, a post office, a railroad station, a store, and a large wooden hotel on the Oceanside of Long Key. The destruction marked the end of an era for this once-prestigious retreat.

Long Key Fishing Club Marker
65700 Overseas Hwy, Layton, FL 33001

**SCAN QR CODE
TO NAVIGATE**

55

BONGO'S BOTANICAL BEER GARDEN AND CAFE

MILEAGE: 114 MI/ 183 KM MARATHON, FL
OVERSEAS HIGHWAY MILE MARKER: 59 MI
24.76975, -80.94058

Bongos stands as a cherished haven among locals, a lush oasis adorned with tropical fruit trees and fragrant herb gardens. They boast an extensive array of more than 20 thoughtfully curated craft beers on tap, complemented by an enticing collection of signature cocktails. Their culinary offerings celebrate the abundance of their 'Grassy Grown' organic fruits, herbs, and the finest local Keez Beez honey, promising a delightful fusion of flavors. Picture yourself gently swaying in our hammock chairs, leisurely strolling through their vibrant botanical garden, or engaging in spirited lawn games—all while indulging in tropical delights harvested directly from their organic garden. Come, be a part of their vibrant community, and let Bongos become your destination for relaxation, revelry, and unforgettable moments.

Bongo's Botanical Beer Garden and Cafe
59300 Overseas Hwy, Marathon, FL 33050

**SCAN QR CODE
TO NAVIGATE**

56

DOLPHIN RESEARCH CENTER

MILEAGE: 114 MI/ 183 KM GRASSY KEY, FL
OVERSEAS HIGHWAY MILE MARKER: 58 MI
24.76697, -80.94550

On your way to Marathon, visit one of the famous dolphin centers in the Florida Keys. Dolphin Research Center (DRC) is a renowned marine mammal facility established in 1984. The center is dedicated to the study, conservation, and education of marine mammals, with a particular emphasis on dolphins. It serves as a unique destination where visitors can interact with and learn about these intelligent and fascinating animals. Visitors to the Dolphin Research Center have the unique opportunity to engage in interactive experiences with dolphins. These experiences may include swimming with dolphins, participating in trainer-for-a-day programs, or attending informative presentations.

Dolphin Research Center
58901 Overseas Hwy, Grassy Key, FL 33050

**SCAN QR CODE
TO NAVIGATE**

☐ TO VISIT
☐ VISITED

57

SUNSET PARK

MILEAGE: 120 MI/ 193 KM KEY COLONY BEACH, FL
OVERSEAS HIGHWAY MILE MARKER: 53 MI
24.71772, -81.02508

I definitely recommend stopping at Sunset Park. It is located on Key Colony Beach, close to Marathon, and offers a picturesque and tranquil setting for visitors seeking a serene retreat in the Florida Keys. Nestled within the charming community of Key Colony Beach, this park is a gem that captivates with its stunning views and recreational opportunities. As the name suggests, Sunset Park is renowned for breathtaking sunset vistas. The park provides an ideal vantage point to witness the sun gracefully descending over the Gulf of Mexico, casting warm hues across the sky and creating a magical ambiance. Visitors often gather here to marvel at the kaleidoscope of colors painting the horizon, making it a perfect spot for a romantic evening or a peaceful moment of reflection. Beyond its sunset allure, Sunset Park offers a pleasant environment for various outdoor activities. The park features well-maintained green spaces, picnic areas, and benches.

Sunset Park
W Ocean Dr, Key Colony Beach, FL 33051

**SCAN QR CODE
TO NAVIGATE**

1

OVERSEAS
HIGHWAY

MARATHON VISITOR CENTER

MILEAGE: 120 MI/ 193 KM MARATHON, FL
OVERSEAS HIGHWAY MILE MARKER: 53 MI
24.73148, -81.02615

Welcome to Marathon! The area that is now Marathon was originally inhabited by Native American tribes, including the Calusa and Tequesta peoples. They lived off the rich marine resources in the region. Spanish explorers, including Juan Ponce de León, were among the first Europeans to visit this area in the early 16th century. During World War II, the Keys became a strategic location for military training and defense. Marathon's airport, now known as the Florida Keys Marathon International Airport, was originally built as a military training facility. In the post-war years, Marathon experienced gradual growth and development. The construction of the Seven Mile Bridge in the 1980s further improved transportation to the area. Before embarking on your Marathon adventure, I highly recommend commencing your journey at the Visitor Center. Here, you'll discover a wealth of essential information, procure a detailed map, and indulge in a visit to their small gift shop.

Greater Marathon Chamber of Commerce & Visitor Center
12222 Overseas Hwy, Marathon, FL 33050

**SCAN QR CODE
TO NAVIGATE**

59

FLORIDA KEYS
AQUARIUM ENCOUNTERS

MILEAGE: 120 MI/ 193 KM MARATHON, FL
OVERSEAS HIGHWAY MILE MARKER: 53 MI
24.73077, -81.03078

Florida Keys Aquarium Encounters offers an engaging marine experience. Dive into a world of wonders as you explore vibrant coral reefs and crystal-clear waters teeming with marine life. The Florida Keys Aquarium Encounters provides an up-close and personal experience with a variety of underwater creatures, from colorful tropical fish to majestic rays and sharks. One of the highlights of your visit is the Coral Reef Encounter, where you can snorkel or dive among the stunning coral formations and interact with an array of marine species. For those seeking a more hands-on experience, the Touch Tank Adventure allows you to feel the unique textures of starfish, sea cucumbers, and other fascinating marine critters. Don't miss the chance to see the Predator Reef Tank, a shark aquarium uniquely situated as an extension of Coral Reef Encounter. I highly recommend visiting this place to witness the beautiful marine life of the Florida Keys.

Florida Keys Aquarium Encounters
11710 Overseas Hwy, Marathon, FL 33050

**SCAN QR CODE
TO NAVIGATE**

TO VISIT
VISITED

60

CURLY'S
COFFEE AND MARINA

MILEAGE: 120 MI/ 193 KM MARATHON, FL
OVERSEAS HIGHWAY MILE MARKER: 53 MI
24.72961, -81.03209

Before we delve further into Marathon, let's take a quick break for coffee at Curly's Coffee and Marina. Locals often say this is one of the best coffee spots in Marathon. Choose from one of their hot coffees, such as a cafe latte, cappuccino, or espresso. Alternatively, you can opt for one of their cold drinks, like iced latte or iced mocha. The beverages are crafted to perfection and rich in flavor. The service is swift and precise, complemented by a convenient walk-up window and a drive-thru option. Outdoor seating is also available for a pleasant and relaxing atmosphere. The area is perfect for a leisurely stroll while enjoying your coffee.

Curly's Coffee and Marina
11601 Overseas Hwy, Marathon, FL 33050

**SCAN QR CODE
TO NAVIGATE**

MARATHON AIR MUSEUM

MILEAGE: 121 MI/ 195 KM MARATHON, FL
OVERSEAS HIGHWAY MILE MARKER: 52 MI
24.72763, -81.04385

In 1940, as the United States prepared for its involvement in World War II, the U.S. government identified the strategic importance of the Florida Keys for military operations. The Marathon Airport was one of the facilities established during this time to support naval aviation training and operations. During the war, the Marathon Airport served as a base for naval air patrol and training missions. The airport's location was advantageous for training pilots in the challenging conditions of the Florida Keys, which included a mix of open water, islands, and diverse weather patterns. Pilots would practice navigation, reconnaissance, and anti-submarine warfare missions in this environment. If you are interested in the history of aviation in this area, as well as modern developments in aviation, I highly recommend visiting the Marathon Air Museum. The museum is free but donations are highly recommended.

Marathon Air Museum
9850 Overseas Hwy, Marathon, FL 33050

SCAN QR CODE
TO NAVIGATE

62

1
OVERSEAS HIGHWAY

FLORIDA EAST COAST OVERSEAS RAILROAD CAR

MILEAGE: 123 MI/ 198 KM MARATHON, FL
OVERSEAS HIGHWAY MILE MARKER: 50 MI
24.71692, -81.07424

Before we delve further into Marathon, let's take a quick break for coffee at Curly's Coffee and Marina. Locals often say this is one of the best coffee spots in Marathon. Choose from one of their hot coffees, such as a cafe latte, cappuccino, or espresso. Alternatively, you can opt for one of their cold drinks, like iced latte or iced mocha. The beverages are crafted to perfection and rich in flavor. The service is swift and precise, complemented by a convenient walk-up window and a drive-thru option. Outdoor seating is also available for a pleasant and relaxing atmosphere. The area is perfect for a leisurely stroll while enjoying your coffee.

Florida East Coast Overseas Railroad Car
5550 Overseas Hwy, Marathon, FL 33050

**SCAN QR CODE
TO NAVIGATE**

6 3

TOURIST ATTRACTION

CRANE POINT HAMMOCK

MILEAGE: 123 MI/ 198 KM MARATHON, FL
OVERSEAS HIGHWAY MILE MARKER: 50 MI

24.71677, -81.07520

In 1940, as the United States prepared for its involvement in World War II, the U.S. government identified the strategic importance of the Florida Keys for military operations. The Marathon Airport was one of the facilities established during this time to support naval aviation training and operations. During the war, the Marathon Airport served as a base for naval air patrol and training missions. The airport's location was advantageous for training pilots in the challenging conditions of the Florida Keys, which included a mix of open water, islands, and diverse weather patterns. Pilots would practice navigation, reconnaissance, and anti-submarine warfare missions in this environment. If you are interested in the history of aviation in this area, as well as modern developments in aviation, I highly recommend visiting the Marathon Air Museum. The museum is free but donations are highly recommended.

Crane Point Hammock
5550 Overseas Hwy, Marathon, FL 33050

**SCAN QR CODE
TO NAVIGATE**

TO VISIT
VISITED

64

 ICONIC PLACE

 NATURAL LANDMARK

 1 OVERSEAS HIGHWAY

SOMBRERO BEACH

MILEAGE: 124 MI/ 200 KM MARATHON, FL
OVERSEAS HIGHWAY MILE MARKER: 49 MI
24.69227, -81.08551

Known for its pristine white sandy shores, crystal-clear turquoise waters, and swaying coconut palms, Sombrero Beach provides a quintessential tropical paradise experience. The beach gets its name from the nearby Sombrero Key, which resembles a sombrero (Spanish for hat). Spanning approximately 12 acres, Sombrero Beach is a public beach maintained by the City of Marathon, making it easily accessible for everyone to enjoy. One of the standout features of Sombrero Beach is its powdery sand, ideal for leisurely strolls, building sandcastles, or simply lounging under the warm Florida sun. The beach is also equipped with picnic areas, pavilions, and barbecue grills, making it a popular spot for family gatherings, picnics, and outdoor celebrations. The shaded pavilions offer respite from the sun, allowing visitors to relax and enjoy breathtaking views of the Atlantic Ocean.

Sombrero Beach
Sombrero Beach Rd, Marathon, FL 33050

**SCAN QR CODE
TO NAVIGATE**

65

KEYS FISHERIES

MILEAGE: 124 MI/ 200 KM MARATHON, FL
OVERSEAS HIGHWAY MILE MARKER: 49 MI
24.71423, -81.09300

When driving through Marathon, it's time for a snack! Don't miss Keys Fisheries, a well-known spot in Marathon for great seafood! Renowned for its fresh seafood, laid-back atmosphere, and stunning waterfront views, this iconic establishment offers a true taste of the Keys' maritime charm. At Keys Fisheries, the menu is a celebration of the ocean's bounty. From succulent stone crab claws to the freshest lobster and shrimp, each dish is a testament to the restaurant's commitment to serving high-quality, locally sourced seafood. The signature "Lobster Reuben" and the mouthwatering "Stone Crab Chowder" are just a couple of the delectable offerings that have earned Keys Fisheries its stellar reputation. In addition to its restaurant, Keys Fisheries boasts a Fresh Market where you can purchase the catch of the day. This market is a treasure trove for seafood enthusiasts, offering an array of fresh fish, stone crab claws, and other local delicacies.

Keys Fisheries
3502 Gulfview Ave, Marathon, FL 33050

**SCAN QR CODE
TO NAVIGATE**

TO VISIT
VISITED

66

 ICONIC PLACE

 TOURIST ATTRACTION

 1 OVERSEAS HIGHWAY

TURTLE HOSPITAL

MILEAGE: 125 MI/ 201 KM MARATHON, FL
OVERSEAS HIGHWAY MILE MARKER: 48 MI
24.70980, -81.10139

The Turtle Hospital in Marathon is dedicated to rescuing and rehabilitating injured sea turtles. Equipped with state-of-the-art facilities and staffed by a team of committed professionals, the hospital focuses on treating various injuries, including boat strikes and entanglement in fishing gear. In addition to rehabilitation, the Turtle Hospital emphasizes education and community outreach, offering guided tours to raise awareness about sea turtle conservation. The facility also conducts public releases of rehabilitated turtles, providing a heartwarming opportunity for visitors to witness these majestic creatures returning to their natural habitat. Through its efforts, the Turtle Hospital plays a crucial role in marine conservation in the Florida Keys.

Turtle Hospital
2396 Overseas Hwy, Marathon, FL 33050

SCAN QR CODE TO NAVIGATE

☐ TO VISIT
☐ VISITED

67

RESTAURANT

1
OVERSEAS
HIGHWAY

SUNSET GRILLE & RAW BAR

MILEAGE: 126 MI / 203 KM MARATHON, FL
OVERSEAS HIGHWAY MILE MARKER: 47 MI
24.70642, -81.12383

Before departing Marathon, I highly recommend paying a visit to Sunset Grille & Raw Bar for an exceptional dining experience with delectable cuisine. Sitting at the foot of the historic 7 Mile Bridge, Sunset Grille offers more than just a dining experience; it's a captivating oceanfront haven. Designed in the style of a charming thatched South Seas tiki hut, the restaurant boasts an expansive oceanfront deck complete with one of the largest pools in the Florida Keys. As you unwind, feel the sand beneath your feet and savor a drink on their relaxing sandy beach. With its prime location, Sunset Grille provides the perfect setting to enjoy both breathtaking sunsets and delightful meals or drinks.

Sunset Grille & Raw Bar
7 Knights Key Blvd, Marathon, FL 33050

**SCAN QR CODE
TO NAVIGATE**

TO VISIT

VISITED

68

 ICONIC PLACE

 TOURIST ATTRACTION

 1
OVERSEAS HIGHWAY

SEVEN MILE BRIDGE

MILEAGE: 126 MI/ 203 KM MARATHON, FL
OVERSEAS HIGHWAY MILE MARKER: 47 MI
24.70726, -81.12294

The Seven Mile Bridge is an iconic and breathtaking structure that spans, as its name suggests, approximately seven miles across the turquoise waters of the Gulf of Mexico. The bridge is renowned not only for its impressive length (the longest bridge in the Florida Keys.) but also for the stunning panoramic views it offers of the surrounding seascape. Completed in 1982, the modern Seven Mile Bridge replaced the original structure. The Old Seven Mile Bridge, a pioneering feat of engineering, was constructed between 1909 and 1912 as part of Henry Flagler's Florida East Coast Railway extension to Key West. The Old Seven Mile Bridge played a vital role in connecting the keys and facilitating transportation in the region. Today, the Old Seven Mile Bridge runs parallel to the modern span and serves a different purpose. While the newer bridge is dedicated to vehicular traffic, the historic structure has been repurposed for recreational activities. It has become a favorite spot for hikers, bikers, and fishing enthusiasts.

7 Mile Bridge - Vista Point
24.70726, -81.12294

**SCAN QR CODE
TO NAVIGATE**

69

QUIRKY ATTRACTION

1
OVERSEAS HIGHWAY

FRED THE TREE

MILEAGE: 131 MI/ 211 KM MARATHON, FL
OVERSEAS HIGHWAY MILE MARKER: 42 MI
24.68955, -81.20483

As you travel across the longest bridge in the Florida Keys, be sure to keep an eye out for one of the quirkier attractions along our journey on the Overseas Highway. Meet Fred, the Australian pine tree that has become a beloved resident of the Old Seven Mile Bridge in the Florida Keys. While the exact origins of Fred remain a mystery, locals estimate that he has been a part of the landscape for around 35 years. Various theories surround Fred's arrival, ranging from the mundane, like bird droppings, to the more elaborate, such as a fortuitous accident involving a truck carrying Australian pine saplings. Despite the state's campaign against non-native pines, Fred has managed to escape the axe, becoming a living testament to resilience. About 14 years ago, a group of locals, affectionately known as Fred's Elves, began adorning him with holiday decorations. Buoys personalized and donated by people, along with a giant solar-powered menorah from a Key West synagogue, transformed Fred into a festive icon. To those who cherish him, Fred is more than just a tree; he's a symbol of resilience and a beacon of hope.

Fred the Tree
24.68955, -81.20483

**SCAN QR CODE
TO NAVIGATE**

*'TO ESCAPE AND SIT QUIETLY ON THE BEACH -
THAT'S MY IDEA OF PARADISE.'*
EMILIA WICKSTEAD

WHERE TO PARK YOUR RV IN LOWER KEYS:

This is a list of recommended RV Parks selected for a safe and comfortable stay:

RV PARKS

Sunshine Key RV Resort and Marina
38801 Overseas Hwy, Big Pine Key, FL 33043

Bahia Honda State Park RV Campground
36850 Overseas Hwy, Big Pine Key, FL 33043

Big Pine Key Resort
33000 Overseas Hwy, Big Pine Key, FL 33043

Royal Palm RV Park
163 Cunningham Ln, Big Pine Key, FL 33043

Sun Outdoors Sugarloaf Key
311 Johnson Rd, Summerland Key, FL 33042

Bluewater Key RV Resort
2950 Overseas Hwy, Key West, FL 33040

WHERE TO STAY IN LOWER KEYS:

RESORTS/HOTELS

Old Wooden Bridge Guest Cottages & Marina
1791 Bogie Dr, Big Pine Key, FL 33043

Little Palm Island Resort & Spa
28500 Overseas Hwy, Little Torch Key, FL 33042

Parmer's Resort
565 Barry Ave, Little Torch Key, FL 33042

Looe Key Reef Resort & Dive Center
27340 Overseas Hwy, Ramrod Key, FL 33042

Venture Out Resort
701 Spanish Main Dr, Cudjoe Key, FL 33042

Sugarloaf Lodge
17001 Overseas Hwy, Sugarloaf Shores, FL 33042

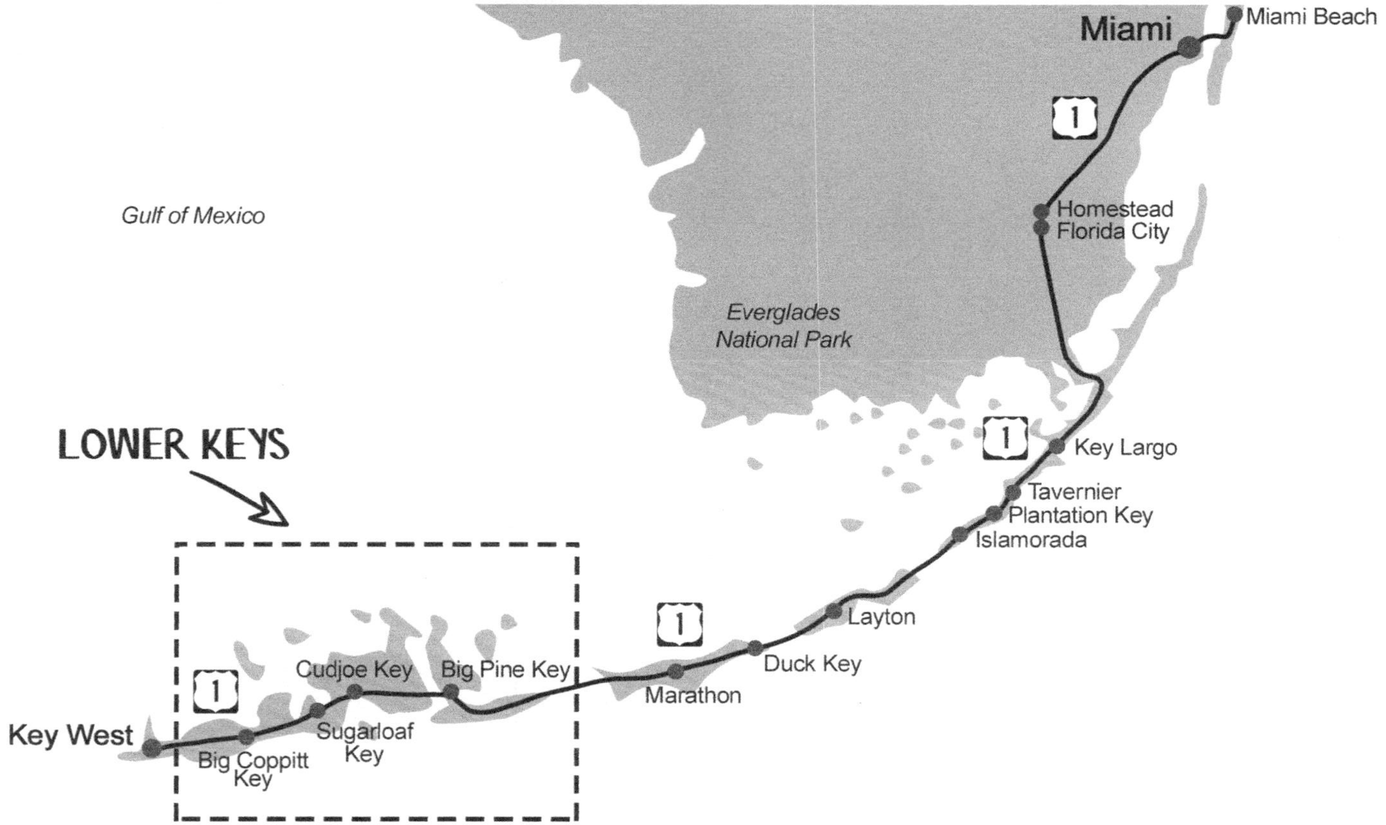
Miami Beach
Miami
1
Gulf of Mexico
Homestead
Florida City
Everglades
National Park
1
Key Largo
Tavernier
Plantation Key
Islamorada
LOWER KEYS
Layton
1
Duck Key
Marathon
Cudjoe Key
Big Pine Key
1
Key West
Sugarloaf
Key
Big Coppitt
Key

PLACES TO VISIT IN LOWER KEYS:

(10) Veterans Memorial Beach

(11) Bahia Honda State Park

(12) Calusa Beach & Loggerhead Beach

(13) Bahia Honda Railroad Bridge

(14) Horseshoe Beach

(15) Key West Visitors Center

(16) National Key Deer Refuge Nature Center

(77) No Name Pub

(78) Blue Hole Observation Platform

(79) Kiki's Sandbar & Grille

(80) Morning Joint

(81) Underwater Photography Gallery

(82) Baby's Coffee

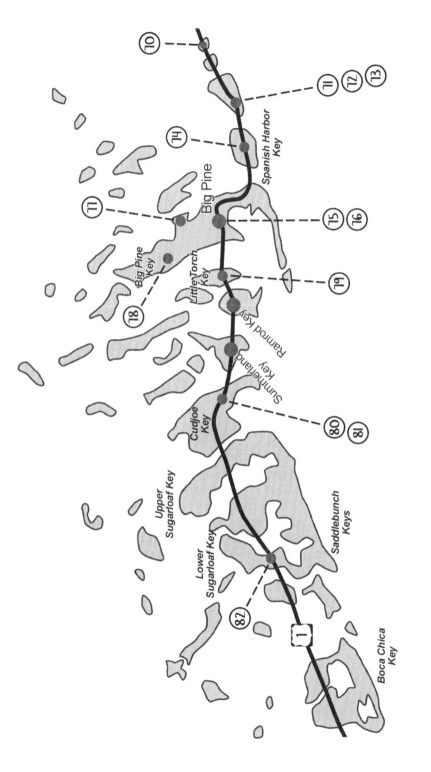

☐ TO VISIT
☐ VISITED

70

VETERANS MEMORIAL BEACH

MILEAGE: 133 MI/ 214 KM LITTLE DUCK KEY, FL
OVERSEAS HIGHWAY MILE MARKER: 39 MI
24.68129, -81.23061

Veterans Memorial Beach is a cozy beach, located right off the highway at the end of the Seven Mile Bridge. This place features tranquil, clear waters, and gentle sandbar walkways through ocean grass. Ideal for families, the comfortable shallows allow for leisurely walks and wildlife encounters, including small fish, crabs, snails, nurse sharks, and jellyfish. Snorkeling enthusiasts will love exploring the natural marine life during high tide, while those with little ones can enjoy the shallow beach during low tide to avoid seaweed at the shoreline. Start your day with a cup of coffee and bask in the awe-inspiring sunrise at this enchanting beach. Whether you prefer the tranquil solitude of a morning stroll or the joy of a picnic with friends, numerous tables provide the perfect vantage point overlooking the sparkling water. Simply pack your favorite snacks and immerse yourself in the beauty of the moment. This beach guarantees an unforgettable experience—where every sunrise and every picnic becomes a cherished memory.

Veterans Memorial Beach
39900 US-1, Big Pine Key, FL 33043

**SCAN QR CODE
TO NAVIGATE**

TO VISIT
VISITED

71

 ICONIC PLACE

 NATURAL LANDMARK

 OVERSEAS HIGHWAY

BAHIA HONDA STATE PARK

MILEAGE: 136 MI/ 219 KM BIG PINE KEY, FL
OVERSEAS HIGHWAY MILE MARKER: 36 MI
24.65822, -81.27677

Welcome to Bahia Honda State Park! One of the park's defining features is its stunning beaches with soft, white sand and crystal-clear turquoise waters. Calusa Beach and Sandspur Beach are two popular stretches of shoreline within the park, offering visitors a tranquil and idyllic setting for sunbathing, swimming, and water activities. The views of the Atlantic Ocean and Gulf of Mexico from the park are simply mesmerizing, making it a favorite destination for nature enthusiasts and photographers. Bahia Honda State Park is also home to a variety of ecosystems, including tropical hardwood hammocks, mangroves, and seagrass beds. The park's rich biodiversity supports a wide range of plant and animal species. An array of recreational activities awaits outdoor enthusiasts. Snorkeling is a popular pastime, as the park's waters are home to vibrant coral reefs and an abundance of marine life. Beyond its natural wonders, Bahia Honda State Park also has historical significance. The park is home to the Bahia Honda Rail Bridge, which was part of Henry Flagler's Overseas Railway in the early 20th century.

Bahia Honda State Park
36850 Overseas Hwy, Big Pine Key, FL 33043

**SCAN QR CODE
TO NAVIGATE**

72

ICONIC PLACE

NATURAL LANDMARK

1
OVERSEAS HIGHWAY

CALUSA BEACH & LOGGERHEAD BEACH

MILEAGE: 136 MI/ 219 KM BIG PINE KEY, FL
OVERSEAS HIGHWAY MILE MARKER: 36 MI
24.65567, -81.27983

Now, let's head to what, in my opinion, is the best beach in Bahia Honda State Park – Calusa Beach. Although the beach isn't very wide, it boasts the best water color and pretty white sand. The water is shallow, making it an excellent spot to hang out. On a non-windy day, it's ideal for families with kids due to its shallow depth. Picnic tables right on the sand make it convenient for enjoying your picnic lunch without going far. Another excellent option for sunbathing is to visit Loggerhead Beach, a long stretch of sand towards the west side of the park. Facing the Atlantic Ocean, it provides more room to stretch. Picnic tables are also available nearby, and on this side, you can engage in other water activities such as kayaking and fishing.

Calusa Beach & Loggerhead Beach
36850 Overseas Hwy, Big Pine Key, FL 33043

**SCAN QR CODE
TO NAVIGATE**

7 3

OLD BAHIA HONDA BRIDGE

MILEAGE: 136 MI/ 219 KM BIG PINE KEY, FL
OVERSEAS HIGHWAY MILE MARKER: 36 MI
24.65473, -81.28170

The Old Bahia Honda Bridge beckons history buffs to explore its fascinating past. Constructed in the early 20th century, the Old Bahia Honda Bridge played a pivotal role in connecting the Florida Keys, providing a lifeline for transportation and commerce. The bridge was originally built by Henry Flagler as part of the Florida East Coast Railway extension, which aimed to connect mainland Florida to Key West. Completed in 1912, the bridge spanned the deep and challenging waters of the Bahia Honda Channel, showcasing the engineering prowess of its time. In 1935, the Labor Day Hurricane, one of the most powerful hurricanes to strike the United States, severely damaged the bridge. The storm wreaked havoc on the Florida Keys and prompted the railroad company to abandon the damaged infrastructure. Following this, the U.S. government acquired the bridge and converted it into a highway bridge. However, its tenure as a crucial transportation link came to an end in 1972 when a new, more modern bridge took over the vehicular traffic.

Bahia Honda Railroad Bridge
Old Bahia Honda Bridge, Big Pine Key, FL 33043

**SCAN QR CODE
TO NAVIGATE**

TO VISIT
VISITED

74

NATURAL LANDMARK

1

OVERSEAS HIGHWAY

HORSESHOE BEACH

MILEAGE: 138 MI / 222 KM BIG PINE KEY, FL
OVERSEAS HIGHWAY MILE MARKER: 35 MI

24.65452, -81.30153

Horseshoe Beach derives its name from the distinctive shape of its shoreline, which closely resembles that of a horseshoe. Originally an old quarry, Horseshoe Beach played an important role in the construction of the iconic Overseas Highway. The coral excavated from its depths was utilized in crafting the foundation of this historic roadway. As a result, the beach bears witness to a tangible piece of the region's transportation history. At the heart of Horseshoe Beach lies a mesmerizing abyss, reaching depths of approximately 30 feet. Adding to the allure of this underwater realm is the rumor of an ambulance submerged within its depths, creating an artificial wreck that captivates the imagination of divers. This unconventional addition to the underwater landscape adds an element of mystery and intrigue to the site.

Horseshoe Beach
1969 Overseas Hwy, Big Pine Key, FL 33043

**SCAN QR CODE
TO NAVIGATE**

75

KEY WEST VISITORS CENTER

MILEAGE: 142 MI/ 229 KM BIG PINE KEY, FL
OVERSEAS HIGHWAY MILE MARKER: 31 MI
24.66895, -81.34233

We still have 31 miles to the center of Key West, but I highly recommend making a stop at the Key West Visitor Center. It's definitely worth checking with them to plan your visit. The Key West Visitor Center serves as a hub for booking guided tours and excursions. Whether you're interested in exploring the historic Old Town, snorkeling in the crystal-clear waters, or taking a sunset cruise, they assist in arranging these activities, ensuring a seamless and enjoyable experience. Additionally, they offer a variety of discounts, coupons, and free maps. Don't forget to check out their small gift shop for souvenirs to commemorate your visit. Taking a brief break at the Key West Visitor Center can enhance your overall journey and help you make the most of your time in this beautiful destination.

Key West Visitors Center
31281 Overseas Hwy, Big Pine Key, FL 33043

**SCAN QR CODE
TO NAVIGATE**

NATIONAL KEY DEER REFUGE NATURE CENTER

MILEAGE: 142 MI/ 229 KM BIG PINE KEY, FL
OVERSEAS HIGHWAY MILE MARKER: 30 MI
24.66979, -81.35451

The National Key Deer Refuge Nature Center stands as a testament to the preservation and protection of one of Florida's most iconic and endangered species, the Key deer (Odocoileus virginianus clavium). Nestled within the lush landscapes of Big Pine Key, this refuge serves as a vital hub for education, conservation, and appreciation of the unique ecosystem that is home to these diminutive deer. The Key deer, a subspecies of white-tailed deer, is found exclusively in the Florida Keys. With a population hovering around a few hundred individuals, the Key deer faces numerous threats, including habitat loss, predation, and collisions with vehicles. The National Key Deer Refuge was established in 1957 to safeguard these animals and their habitat, ensuring the survival of this remarkable species for generations to come.

National Key Deer Refuge Nature Center
30587 Overseas Hwy, Big Pine Key, FL 33043

**SCAN QR CODE
TO NAVIGATE**

☐ TO VISIT
☐ VISITED

77

NO NAME PUB

MILEAGE: 143 MI/ 230 KM BIG PINE KEY, FL
OVERSEAS HIGHWAY MILE MARKER: 30 MI
24.69812, -81.35123

Nestled on Big Pine Key, the No Name Pub boasts a rich history dating back to 1931. Initially a humble general store and bait and tackle shop, it underwent a transformation in 1936 when a small room was added, birthing the iconic restaurant and pub we know today. In its early years, No Name Pub welcomed patrons from diverse backgrounds, including world travelers arriving via ferry from the mainland and local fishermen. The late 1930s marked a unique chapter in the pub's history when the owners, in a bid to boost business, converted the upstairs storage room into a brothel. Although short-lived, this intriguing venture added an unexpected twist to the establishment's narrative. Presenting a menu that is a testament to its time-honored legacy, No Name Pub offers the best pizza anywhere, mouthwatering chili, delectable smoked fish dip, and sandwiches served on quaint paper plates. The ambiance is a genuine throwback, featuring an old rustic bar adorned with autographed dollar bills, creating a charming and laid-back atmosphere.

No Name Pub
30813 Watson Blvd, Big Pine Key, FL 33043

**SCAN QR CODE
TO NAVIGATE**

78

BLUE HOLE
OBSERVATION PLATFORM

MILEAGE: 143 MI/ 230 KM BIG PINE KEY, FL
OVERSEAS HIGHWAY MILE MARKER: 30 MI
24.70594, -81.37999

The Blue Hole Observation Platform offers a captivating blend of natural beauty and wildlife encounters, making it an ideal spot for visitors of all ages and abilities to connect with the great outdoors. Originally a limestone quarry, the Blue Hole has undergone a transformation into a freshwater haven, now adorned with native plants that provide a serene and shaded environment. Accessible to everyone, a short and paved trail leads from the parking lot to the observation platform, ensuring a comfortable journey for all. As you traverse the trail, be prepared for a delightful rendezvous with native wildlife. The Blue Hole is home to an array of fascinating species, including the iconic American alligator, the majestic osprey, graceful green herons, and other captivating wading birds. Keep your eyes peeled for the anhinga, magnificent frigatebirds, white-crowned pigeon, white-eyed vireo, and the lively blue-gray gnatcatcher, among many others.

Blue Hole Observation Platform
Key Deer Blvd, Big Pine Key, FL 33043

**SCAN QR CODE
TO NAVIGATE**

79

KIKI'S SANDBAR & GRILLE

MILEAGE: 145 MI/ 233 KM LITTLE TORCH KEY, FL
OVERSEAS HIGHWAY MILE MARKER: 28 MI
24.66905, -81.38732

Discover the ultimate beachfront oasis at Kiki's Sandbar, where the essence of seaside living meets culinary excellence. Indulge in the freshest seafood, expertly crafted drinks, and nightly live music, creating an unforgettable experience for every visitor. With its beachside Tiki Bar, playful games beach, and inviting Raw Bar, Kiki's offers a perfect blend of relaxation and excitement. Ascend to the upstairs air-conditioned dining room for a delightful meal, served daily for lunch and dinner. Whether you arrive by land or sea, Kiki's Sandbar promises an incredible atmosphere, with panoramic views overlooking the enchanting Newfound and Marsch Harbors. Immerse yourself in the coastal charm and culinary delights that define Kiki's Sandbar – a destination that captures the spirit of seaside living.

Kiki's Sandbar & Grille
183 Barry Ave, Little Torch Key, FL 33042

**SCAN QR CODE
TO NAVIGATE**

80

MORNING JOINT

MILEAGE: 150 MI/ 241 KM CUDJOE KEY, FL
OVERSEAS HIGHWAY MILE MARKER: 22 MI
24.66279, -81.47722

Let's take a quick break for coffee. Morning Joint Cafe offers a welcoming haven where guests are treated like family, embodying their vision of hospitality. The ambiance is carefully crafted to provide a comfortable and relaxing experience for everyone who steps through the doors. Indulge in the delightful array of made-to-order Munchies, savor the farm-to-table Colombian Coffee, and treat yourself to a cheat day with their irresistibly fresh pastries. One of the unique charms of Morning Joint is its pet-friendly back patio, providing the perfect setting to enjoy the beautiful Florida Keys weather while sipping on your favorite brew or nibbling on a tasty treat. Whether you're a local or a visitor, the cafe invites you to stop in and make yourself at home, creating memorable moments in the heart of their warm and inviting space. In addition to their culinary offerings, Morning Joint boasts a small merchandising gift shop. Here, you can explore a curated selection of items that capture the essence of the cafe's spirit, making it easy to take a piece of the experience home with you.

Morning Joint
22864 Overseas Hwy, Cudjoe Key, FL 33042

**SCAN QR CODE
TO NAVIGATE**

81

TOURIST ATTRACTION

OVERSEAS HIGHWAY

UNDERWATER PHOTOGRAPHY GALLERY

MILEAGE: 150 MI/ 241 KM CUDJOE KEY, FL
OVERSEAS HIGHWAY MILE MARKER: 22 MI
24.66307, -81.48137

This little photography gallery is well worth a stop. Founded by the passionate duo Michael and Suzanne Lombard, this intimate gallery offers a captivating glimpse into the mesmerizing world beneath the ocean's surface. With over 40 years of diving and photographing experience worldwide, the Lombard family is a testament to a profound love for underwater exploration. The gallery showcases several dozen photographs that vividly portray the breathtaking beauty of underwater life. As you step into this small yet enchanting space, you'll find yourself immersed in a world of vibrant colors, diverse marine species, and the sheer wonder of the ocean's depths. The Lombard family's dedication to ocean conservation echoes through their work. Their lens captures not only the awe-inspiring scenes of marine life but also serves as a powerful advocate for the recovery of threatened and endangered species.

Underwater Photography Gallery
22627 La Fitte Dr, Cudjoe Key, FL 33042

SCAN QR CODE TO NAVIGATE

TO VISIT
VISITED

82

BABY'S COFFEE

MILEAGE: 158 MI/ 254 KM KEY WEST, FL
OVERSEAS HIGHWAY MILE MARKER: 15 MI
24.62861, -81.59284

Welcome to the enchanting world of Baby's Coffee, a journey that began in 1991 when Gary and Olga traded the hustle and bustle of New York for the laid-back charm of Key West, Florida. Nestled on the uptown side of Duval Street, their small coffee roasting company found a home with a rich history. Picture this: In the 1920s, the very building you're standing in was owned by an old Cuban family who lovingly called it "Baby's Place" after their youngest son. "Baby" Rodriguez, all grown up, ran a lively cantina here. Legend has it that literary giant Ernest Hemingway engaged in friendly games of chance with the locals, affectionately known as "conchs." Inspired by the captivating history of this locale, Gary and Olga embraced the name "Baby's" and opened the doors to Baby's Coffee. As you sip your freshly brewed cup, you're not just enjoying the rich aroma; you're immersing yourself in a story that spans generations. Oh, and don't forget to visit their small gift shop inside! They have great T-shirts!

Baby's Coffee
3180 US Highway 1 MM 15, Key West, FL 33040

**SCAN QR CODE
TO NAVIGATE**

"KEY WEST IS NOT JUST A PLACE ON THE MAP; IT'S A STATE OF MIND, A HAVEN WHERE THE SUN KISSES YOUR SOUL, AND TIME DANCES TO THE RHYTHM OF THE WAVES."

UNKNOWN

WELCOME TO THE
KEY WEST AREA

WHERE TO PARK YOUR RV IN THE KEY WEST AREA:

This is a list of recommended RV Parks selected for a safe and comfortable stay:

RV PARKS

RV Key West - Rent RV Lots
55 Boca Chica Rd, Key West, FL 33040

Geiger Key Marina, RV Park & Fish Camp
5 Geiger Rd, Key West, FL 33040

El Mar RV Resort
6700 Maloney Ave, Key West, FL 33040

Boyd's Key West Campground
6401 Maloney Ave, Key West, FL 33040

Leo's Campground and RV Park
5264 Suncrest Rd, Key West, FL 33040

Sigsbee Campground
Arthur Sawyer Dr, Key West, FL 33040

WHERE TO STAY IN THE KEY WEST AREA:

RESORTS/HOTELS

Oceans Edge Resort & Marina Key West
5950 Peninsular Ave, Key West, FL 33040

The Perry Hotel & Marina Key West
7001 Shrimp Rd, Naval Air Station Key West, FL 33040

Havana Cabana Key West
3420 N Roosevelt Blvd, Key West, FL 33040

The Capitana Key West
2401 N Roosevelt Blvd, Key West, FL 33040

Ocean Key Resort & Spa
0 Duval St, Key West, FL 33040

Opal Key Resort & Marina
245 Front St, Key West, FL 33040

Southernmost Beach Resort
1319 Duval St, Key West, FL 33040

Sunset Key Cottages
245 Front St, Key West, FL 33040

Miami Beach

Miami

Homestead
Florida City

Everglades
National Park

Key Largo

Tavernier
Plantation Key
Islamorada

Layton

Duck Key

Marathon

Big Pine Key

Gulf of Mexico

Cudjoe Key

Sugarloaf
Key

Big Coppitt
Key

KEY WEST
AREA

Key West

PLACES TO VISIT IN THE KEY WEST AREA:

(83) Hogfish Bar & Grill

(84) The Docks Restaurant + Raw Bar

(85) Fort East Martello Museum

(86) Smathers Beach

(87) Edward B. Knight Pier

(88) Southernmost Point of the Continental U.S.A.

(89) The Key West Butterfly and Nature Conservatory

(90) Key West Lighthouse

(91) The Hemingway Home and Museum

(92) Fort Zachary Taylor Historic State Park

(93) USCGC Ingham Maritime Museum

(94) Truman Little White House

(95) Mel Fisher Maritime Museum

(96) Key West Shipwreck Museum

(97) Key West Aquarium

(98) Sunset Celebration at Mallory Square

(99) Yankee Freedom Dry Tortugas Ferry

(100) Duval Street

(101) Mile Marker 0 Sign

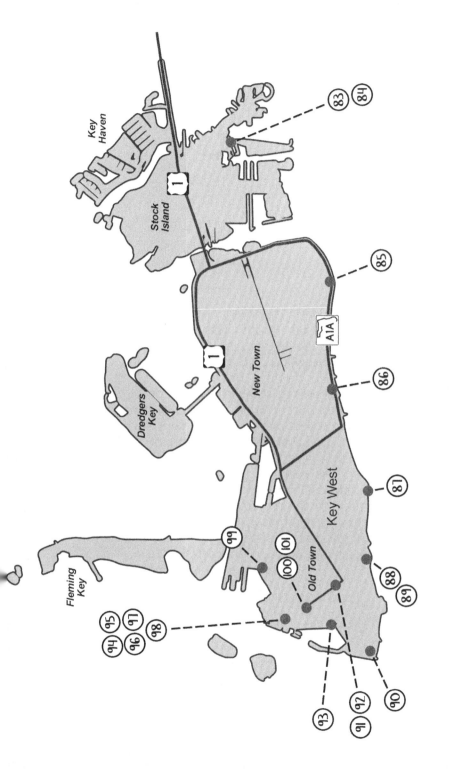

83

HOGFISH BAR & GRILL

MILEAGE: 168 MI/ 270 KM STOCK ISLAND, FL
OVERSEAS HIGHWAY MILE MARKER: 5 MI
24.56629, -81.73340

Before we arrive in Key West, I highly recommend grabbing a bite at Hogfish Bar & Grill. This is not a typical tourist stop. It's a genuine locals' spot that bypasses the pretension and hype found elsewhere, offering a refreshing escape into the heart of the Florida Keys' rich maritime culture. At Hogfish Bar & Grill, time seems to stand still as you delve into a world where fresh seafood, potent drinks, and captivating waterfront views take center stage. As you make your way to the entrance, the inviting aroma of the day's catch, straight from the boats to your plate, sets the stage for a culinary experience unlike any other. The menu is a testament to their commitment to quality, showcasing the freshest local seafood in dishes that pay homage to the region's maritime heritage. From succulent shrimp to the most flavorful fish, each bite is a journey into the authentic flavors of the Keys. Take a seat outdoors and let the laid-back ambiance transport you to a place where life is enjoyed at a slower pace.

Hogfish Bar & Grill
6810 Front St, Stock Island, FL 33040

**SCAN QR CODE
TO NAVIGATE**

84

THE DOCKS
RESTAURANT + RAW BAR

MILEAGE: 168 MI/ 270 KM STOCK ISLAND, FL
OVERSEAS HIGHWAY MILE MARKER: 5 MI
24.56500, -81.73345

Another fantastic dining option in this area is The Docks Restaurant + Raw Bar. Nestled away from the bustling old town of Key West, The Docks Restaurant + Raw Bar offers a delightful escape marked by tasty drinks, delectable dinners, and indulgent desserts provided with impeccable service against a backdrop of scenic views. The atmosphere is a perfect blend of relaxation and cleanliness, creating an enjoyable dining experience. The menu boasts a diverse array of culinary delights, with highlights such as the Fresh Oysters stealing the spotlight for seafood enthusiasts. The Cauliflower Seafood Parmesan Bake is a culinary masterpiece, providing a unique and satisfying dining experience. Paired with a selection of cold drinks, the overall dining experience is elevated to perfection.

The Docks Restaurant + Raw Bar
6840 Front St, Key West, FL 33040

**SCAN QR CODE
TO NAVIGATE**

FORT EAST MARTELLO MUSEUM

MILEAGE: 170 MI/ 274 KM KEY WEST, FL
OVERSEAS HIGHWAY MILE MARKER: 3 MI
24.55209, -81.75521

Welcome to Key West! We've finally arrived at this vibrant and picturesque island at the southernmost tip of the United States. Did you know that Key West once seceded from the United States and declared itself the Conch Republic in 1982? While it was a playful and symbolic act, the Conch Republic has since become a beloved part of Key West's identity. Look out for Conch Republic flags and memorabilia as you explore the island. But first, let's delve into Key West's intriguing history at the Fort East Martello Museum. This well-preserved Civil War-era fort turned museum offers a fascinating glimpse into the island's past. Constructed during the Civil War but never completed, Fort East Martello now houses a treasure trove of historical artifacts, including relics from the wreck of the Isaac Allerton, a ship that sank off the coast of Key West in 1856. As you wander through the corridors, you'll encounter exhibits on military history, local maritime heritage, and the diverse cultures that have shaped Key West.

Fort East Martello Museum
3501 S Roosevelt Blvd, Key West, FL 33040

**SCAN QR CODE
TO NAVIGATE**

TO VISIT
VISITED

86

 ICONIC PLACE

 NATURAL LANDMARK

 1 OVERSEAS HIGHWAY

SMATHERS BEACH

MILEAGE: 171 MI/ 275 KM KEY WEST, FL
OVERSEAS HIGHWAY MILE MARKER: 2 MI
24.55198, -81.76873

After an enriching museum experience, it's time to bask in the sunshine and enjoy the tropical beauty of Key West at Smathers Beach. Located on the southern side of the island, Smathers Beach is renowned for its long stretch of soft, sandy shoreline and crystal-clear turquoise waters. As you arrive, you'll be greeted by swaying palm trees and the inviting sound of gentle waves. Smathers Beach was named after George A. Smathers, a former United States Senator from Florida, who served from 1951 to 1969. The beach was dedicated to him in recognition of his contributions to the state. The fine, white sand at Smathers Beach is not native to the area. In the 1950s, the beach underwent a significant project that involved importing sand from the Caribbean to create the beautiful coastline that visitors enjoy today. Whether you're seeking relaxation, adventure, or a bit of both, Smathers Beach provides the perfect backdrop for a memorable Key West experience.

Smathers Beach
2601 S Roosevelt Blvd, Key West, FL 33040

**SCAN QR CODE
TO NAVIGATE**

TO VISIT
VISITED

87

1

OVERSEAS HIGHWAY

EDWARD B. KNIGHT PIER

MILEAGE: 172 MI/ 277 KM   KEY WEST, FL
OVERSEAS HIGHWAY MILE MARKER: 1 MI
24.54643, -81.78392

The Edward B. Knight Pier, affectionately known as the Key West Pier, stands as a historic and beloved landmark in the heart of Key West. Its origins trace back to the late 1800s when it was initially erected as a shipping dock, serving a crucial role in the maritime activities that shaped the region's development. Over the years, the pier underwent a remarkable transformation, evolving from a utilitarian port into a multifaceted hub for recreation and tourism. Named after Edward B. Knight, a pivotal figure in Key West's early 20th-century development, the pier carries not only physical but historical weight, giving testament to the city's maritime heritage. One notable feature at the entrance of the pier is the Key West Aids Memorial, a poignant reminder of the challenges and losses faced by the community in the face of the AIDS epidemic. This memorial serves as a tribute to those who have been affected, a place for reflection, and a symbol of resilience within the vibrant Key West community.

Edward B. Knight Pier
White St, Key West, FL 33040

**SCAN QR CODE
TO NAVIGATE**

TO VISIT
VISITED

88

ICONIC
PLACE

TOURIST
ATTRACTION

OVERSEAS
HIGHWAY

SOUTHERNMOST POINT OF THE CONTINENTAL U.S.A.

MILEAGE: 173 MI/ 278 KM KEY WEST, FL
OVERSEAS HIGHWAY MILE MARKER: 0 MI
24.54650, -81.79751

An absolute must-see point during your Overseas Highway journey and also the most popular tourist stop on Key West. The Southernmost Point of the Continental U.S.A. is an iconic landmark marked by a large, colorful buoy. Positioned at the intersection of Whitehead Street and South Street, the buoy is a popular destination for people seeking a memorable photo opportunity. The buoy is painted with vibrant colors and adorned with the words "Southernmost Point, Continental U.S.A.," making it easily recognizable. You can line up to capture pictures with this distinctive marker, which has become an iconic symbol of Key West's geographical significance. This point is just 90 miles (145 kilometers) from the northern coast of Cuba. This proximity highlights the geographic and cultural connections between Key West and the Caribbean.

Southernmost Point of the Continental U.S.A.
1400 Whitehead St, Key West, FL 33040

**SCAN QR CODE
TO NAVIGATE**

89

THE KEY WEST BUTTERFLY AND NATURE CONSERVATORY

MILEAGE: 173 MI/ 278 KM KEY WEST, FL
OVERSEAS HIGHWAY MILE MARKER: 0 MI
24.54755, -81.79683

Are you a fan of nature? Don't miss The Key West Butterfly and Nature Conservatory during your visit. This enchanting destination offers a unique and immersive experience, allowing you to witness the delicate dance of butterflies while surrounded by lush tropical gardens. One of the highlights of the conservatory is the butterfly habitat, a carefully controlled environment that mimics the conditions of a tropical rainforest. The conservatory is housed in a distinctive glass structure that allows you to step into a world of vibrant colors and fluttering wings. As you enter, the gentle hum of butterflies in flight and the sweet fragrance of blooming flowers greets you. The main atrium is a breathtaking space filled with tropical plants, cascading waterfalls, and a profusion of nectar-rich flowers that attract the resident butterflies.

The Key West Butterfly and Nature Conservatory
1316 Duval St, Key West, FL 33040

**SCAN QR CODE
TO NAVIGATE**

TO VISIT

VISITED

90

ICONIC PLACE

HISTORICAL LANDMARK

1
OVERSEAS HIGHWAY

KEY WEST LIGHTHOUSE

MILEAGE: 173 MI/ 278 KM KEY WEST, FL

OVERSEAS HIGHWAY MILE MARKER: 0 MI

24.55045, -81.80068

The Key West Lighthouse is a historic maritime landmark with a rich history. Built in 1848, the 65-foot tower replaced an earlier structure to improve visibility. Its distinctive black and white colors make it easily recognizable. Over the years, it served as a crucial navigational aid, manned by dedicated lighthouse keepers. Despite being decommissioned in 1969, the Key West Art & Historical Society restored and preserved the lighthouse, turning it into a museum. It now offers visitors a chance to climb to the top and enjoy panoramic views. The museum showcases exhibits on Key West's maritime history, the lives of lighthouse keepers, and the importance of lighthouses in general.

Key West Lighthouse
938 Whitehead St, Key West, FL 33040

SCAN QR CODE TO NAVIGATE

THE HEMINGWAY HOME AND MUSEUM

MILEAGE: 173 MI/ 278 KM KEY WEST, FL
OVERSEAS HIGHWAY MILE MARKER: 0 MI
24.55114, -81.80064

Embarking on a journey through the enchanting streets of Key West, one must not overlook the allure of a must-see and iconic point—the Hemingway Home and Museum. The house, a Spanish colonial style mansion, was constructed in 1851 and once served as the home of the renowned American author Ernest Hemingway. Hemingway and his second wife, Pauline Pfeiffer, moved into the residence in 1931. Hemingway lived here for almost a decade, during which he wrote some of his most famous works, including "The Old Man and the Sea", "Green Hills of Africa", and "For Whom the Bell Tolls". One of the notable features of the Hemingway Home is its lush and picturesque gardens, home to a colony of six-toed cats. Legend has it that a ship's captain gave Hemingway a six-toed cat and today, descendants of that original feline inhabit the property. These unique cats have become a symbol of the museum and are often referred to as "Hemingway cats".

The Hemingway Home and Museum
907 Whitehead St, Key West, FL 33040

**SCAN QR CODE
TO NAVIGATE**

92

FORT ZACHARY TAYLOR
HISTORIC STATE PARK

MILEAGE: 174 MI/ 280 KM KEY WEST, FL
OVERSEAS HIGHWAY MILE MARKER: 0 MI
24.54652, -81.81061

Fort Zachary Taylor Historic State Park offers visitors a unique blend of cultural heritage, military history, and recreational opportunities. At the heart of the park is Fort Zachary Taylor, a historic military fortress named after President Zachary Taylor, which played a vital role in American history. Constructed between 1845 and 1866, the fort served as a strategic outpost during the Civil War and the Spanish-American War. Its massive walls, brick arches, and gun emplacements provide a glimpse into the challenges and triumphs of the past. Guided tours and interpretive displays within the fort offer a fascinating journey through time, allowing visitors to understand its role in shaping the nation's history. Don't forget to visit one of the main attractions of the park! Its stunning beach is widely regarded as one of the best in Key West!

Fort Zachary Taylor Historic State Park
601 Howard England Way, Key West, FL 33040

**SCAN QR CODE
TO NAVIGATE**

93

USCGC INGHAM
MARITIME MUSEUM

MILEAGE: 174 MI/ 280 KM KEY WEST, FL
OVERSEAS HIGHWAY MILE MARKER: 0 MI
24.55220, -81.80777

Our next great stop in Key West is the USCGC Ingham Maritime Museum. The museum is housed aboard the historic USCGC Ingham, a decommissioned United States Coast Guard Cutter that served for several decades. As you explore the museum, you'll discover the rich legacy of this historic vessel and learn about its service in various missions, including search and rescue operations, law enforcement, and defense efforts. The museum showcases artifacts, exhibits, and interactive displays that chronicle the ship's remarkable journeys and contributions to safeguarding the United States' coastlines. Be sure to take your time exploring the different sections of the vessel, from the well-preserved ship compartments to the informative exhibits that detail the life and duties of the Coast Guard crew.

USCGC Ingham Maritime Museum
Southard St, Key West, FL 33041

**SCAN QR CODE
TO NAVIGATE**

MUSEUM

TRUMAN LITTLE WHITE HOUSE

MILEAGE: 175 MI/ 282 KM KEY WEST, FL
OVERSEAS HIGHWAY MILE MARKER: 0 MI
24.55625, -81.80688

History buffs don't miss this point in our journey! This historic site served as the winter White House for President Harry S. Truman during his presidency. The Truman Little White House offers visitors a unique glimpse into the life and times of one of America's most influential leaders. Step into the very rooms where President Truman made crucial decisions and hosted important meetings. The house has been meticulously preserved, allowing you to immerse yourself in the historical ambiance of the mid-20th century. As you wander through the various rooms, you'll encounter artifacts, photographs, and exhibits that tell the story of Truman's presidency. Learn about the challenges and triumphs of the post-World War II era and gain insights into the political landscape of the time.

Truman Little White House
111 Front St, Naval Air Station Key West, FL 33040

**SCAN QR CODE
TO NAVIGATE**

MUSEUM

1
OVERSEAS
HIGHWAY

MEL FISHER
MARITIME MUSEUM

MILEAGE: 175 MI/ 282 KM   KEY WEST, FL
OVERSEAS HIGHWAY MILE MARKER: 0 MI
24.55804, -81.80648

The Mel Fisher Maritime Museum is a renowned institution dedicated to preserving and showcasing the maritime history of the region, with a particular emphasis on shipwrecks and underwater archaeology. The museum was established in 1982 by Mel Fisher and his family. Mel Fisher was a pioneer in the field of marine archaeology and is best known for discovering the Atocha, a Spanish treasure galleon that sank off the Florida Keys in 1622. The Atocha discovery yielded an incredible amount of gold, silver, and other valuable artifacts, making it one of the most significant underwater archaeological finds in history. The museum houses a diverse collection of artifacts retrieved from various shipwrecks in the waters surrounding Florida and the Caribbean. The exhibits include treasures, coins, and jewelry, providing visitors with a glimpse into the rich maritime history of the region. A major highlight of the museum is the Atocha exhibit, where visitors can marvel at the treasures recovered from the sunken galleon.

Mel Fisher Maritime Museum
200 Greene St, Key West, FL 33040

**SCAN QR CODE
TO NAVIGATE**

96

KEY WEST
SHIPWRECK MUSEUM

MILEAGE: 175 MI/ 282 KM KEY WEST, FL
OVERSEAS HIGHWAY MILE MARKER: 0 MI
24.55903, -81.80690

The Key West Shipwreck Museum offers visitors a captivating journey into the maritime history of this tropical paradise. Located in the heart of Old Town Key West, this museum transports guests back to the 19th century, when the treacherous waters surrounding the island made shipwrecks a common occurrence. Housed in a meticulously recreated wrecker's warehouse, the museum provides a hands-on and immersive experience. Through interactive exhibits, artifacts, and storytelling, visitors gain insight into the lives of the brave wreckers who salvaged valuable cargo. The museum's centerpiece is the 65-foot lookout tower, offering panoramic views of the island and the Gulf of Mexico, just as the original wreckers would have surveyed the horizon for incoming vessels.

Key West Shipwreck Museum
1 Whitehead St, Key West, FL 33040

**SCAN QR CODE
TO NAVIGATE**

97

TOURIST ATTRACTION

1
OVERSEAS HIGHWAY

KEY WEST AQUARIUM

MILEAGE: 175 MI/ 282 KM KEY WEST, FL
OVERSEAS HIGHWAY MILE MARKER: 0 MI
24.55906, -81.80733

Continuing on our journey, we find ourselves drawn to the allure of the ocean depths. The Key West Aquarium, nestled in the heart of Mallory Square, invites curious souls to embark on an aquatic voyage like no other. A historic landmark with roots tracing back to 1934, the aquarium is a living window into the enchanting underwater world of the Florida Keys. Venturing into the aquarium, visitors are greeted by a kaleidoscope of marine wonders. Tanks teem with colorful coral reefs and schools of tropical fish gracefully weave through underwater landscapes. It's a mesmerizing experience that bridges the gap between the island's vibrant streets and the tranquil depths of the ocean. The aquarium's diverse exhibits showcase the unique marine ecosystems that surround Key West. From seahorses swaying gently in the currents to graceful sea turtles gliding through the water, each resident of the aquarium contributes to the narrative of the ocean's delicate balance.

Key West Aquarium
1 Whitehead St, Key West, FL 33040

**SCAN QR CODE
TO NAVIGATE**

98

SUNSET CELEBRATION
MALLORY SQUARE

MILEAGE: 175 MI/ 282 KM KEY WEST, FL
OVERSEAS HIGHWAY MILE MARKER: 0 MI
24.55994, -81.80771

The Sunset Celebration at Mallory Square is a renowned and beloved tradition in Key West. Each evening, locals and visitors gather at Mallory Square, a historic waterfront plaza, to witness one of nature's most breathtaking spectacles—the sunset over the Gulf of Mexico. This daily event has become a vibrant and festive occasion that captures the spirit of Key West's laid-back and artistic community. The Sunset Celebration typically begins a couple of hours before sunset, as performers, artisans, and vendors start setting up their stalls along the square. Mallory Square comes alive with the sounds of live music, street performers, and the chatter of excited onlookers. The atmosphere is infused with a palpable sense of anticipation and celebration. Whether you're a first-time visitor or a seasoned local, the Sunset Celebration offers a daily dose of joy, inspiration, and connection as the sun sets on the southernmost point of the United States.

Sunset Celebration at Mallory Square
Mallory Square Pier, 420 Wall St, Key West, FL 33040

**SCAN QR CODE
TO NAVIGATE**

99

DRY TORTUGAS NATIONAL PARK

MILEAGE: 176 MI/ 283 KM KEY WEST, FL
OVERSEAS HIGHWAY MILE MARKER: 0 MI
24.56250, -81.79889

Dry Tortugas National Park is a captivating and remote gem located in the Gulf of Mexico, approximately 70 miles west of Key West. It is home to crystal-clear waters, vibrant coral reefs, and a historic fortress, making it a must-visit destination for nature enthusiasts and history buffs alike. At the heart of the park stands Fort Jefferson, an imposing 19th-century coastal fortress built to protect strategic shipping routes in the Gulf of Mexico. The largest brick masonry structure in the Americas, Fort Jefferson has a storied past, serving as a military prison during the Civil War. Visitors can explore the fort's extensive grounds, discover its history through interpretive exhibits, and marvel at its architectural grandeur. One of the most convenient ways to experience this tropical haven is through the Yankee Freedom Dry Tortugas Ferry, offering daily excursions from Key West to the park.

Yankee Freedom Dry Tortugas Ferry
100 Grinnell St, Key West, FL 33040

**SCAN QR CODE
TO NAVIGATE**

100

DUVAL STREET

MILEAGE: 177 MI / 285 KM KEY WEST, FL
OVERSEAS HIGHWAY MILE MARKER: 0 MI
24.55908, -81.80523

As our journey nears its end, let's make our way to vibrant Duval Street, a lively thoroughfare nestled in the heart of Key West. Known for its eclectic mix of shops, cafes, and eateries, Duval Street promises a delightful blend of history, culture, and entertainment. As you stroll along this iconic street, you'll discover its rich history, dating back to the early 19th century when Key West was a bustling port city. Named after Florida's first territorial governor, William Pope Duval, the street has witnessed the ebb and flow of time, evolving into the bustling hub it is today. As hunger beckons, Duval Street boasts an array of dining options, from seafood shacks serving up the catch of the day to upscale restaurants offering a taste of Key West's culinary delights. Let's find a cozy spot to savor some delicious coffee or indulge in a meal that captures the essence of the island.

Duval St
Duval St, Key West, FL 33040

**SCAN QR CODE
TO NAVIGATE**

101

MILE MARKER 0 SIGN

MILEAGE: 178 MI/ 286 KM KEY WEST, FL
OVERSEAS HIGHWAY MILE MARKER: 0 MI
24.55514, -81.80382

As you stand before the Mile Marker 0 Sign in Key West, a wave of accomplishment washes over you. This iconic landmark signifies the end of a remarkable journey along the Overseas Highway, a road that weaves through the breathtaking beauty of the Florida Keys. Don't miss the opportunity to explore the Zero Mile Art gift shop located adjacent to the marker. It adds a delightful touch to your experience. In my opinion, it is one of the best gift shops along the entire Overseas Highway. Congratulations on reaching this symbolic milestone! As you bask in the glory of Mile Marker 0, let the tropical vibes of Key West embrace you. The vibrant atmosphere, the laid-back charm, and the promise of endless fun await. Your arrival marks not just the end of a journey but the beginning of an exciting chapter in Key West. So, revel in the island spirit, savor the sunset, and let the celebration begin! Wishing you an amazing adventure in Key West and I can't wait to reunite on our next adventure!

Zero Mile Art
501 Whitehead St Suite 1, Key West, FL 33040

**SCAN QR CODE
TO NAVIGATE**

CONGRATULATIONS

OVERSEAS
HIGHWAY
TRAVELER

....
(Your name, nickname)

This person traveled across the Overseas Highway

Start date.......................................

Finish date......................................

Total days.......................................

Total Places visited............................

ABOUT THE AUTHOR:

Mark Watson is a member of a Los Angeles Motorcycle Club and an avid traveler based in California. Having ridden his Harley-Davidson along the entire length of the Overseas Highway multiple times, he knows the road like the back of his hand. He is also a bestselling author on Amazon, with other popular travel guides: "Route 66 Travel Guide - 202 Amazing Places", "Alaska Highway Travel Guide - 202 Best Stops", and "Pacific Coast Highway Travel Guide - 202 Best Stops."

PLEASE RATE THIS BOOK AND ADD A REVIEW IF YOU ENJOYED IT. THIS WILL REWARD ALL THE HARD WORK PUT INTO THIS TRAVEL GUIDE AND HELP OTHERS ALL OVER THE WORLD START THEIR OWN JOURNEY ON THE OVERSEAS HIGHWAY. IF YOU ENCOUNTER ANY ISSUES OR HAVE CONCERNS ABOUT THE BOOK, PLEASE DON'T HESITATE TO REACH OUT TO ME.

DON'T FORGET TO ADD HASHTAG:#MARKWATSONTRAVELER IF YOU SHARE PHOTOS OR VIDEOS ON SOCIAL MEDIA.

FOR BUSINESS AND PRIVATE INQUIRIES, PLEASE CONTACT:

MARKWATSONTRAVELER@GMAIL.COM

MARKWATSON.TRAVELER

WWW.MARKWATSONTRAVELER.COM

CHECK OUT MY OTHER BOOKS
AVAILABLE FOR SALE ON AMAZON

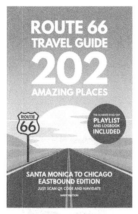

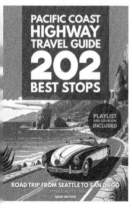

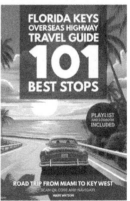

OVERSEAS HIGHWAY

TRAVEL JOURNAL
LOGBOOK

DAY NUMBER.......... DATE..................

STARTING POINT: .... MILEAGE ☐☐☐☐

ENDING POINT: .... MILEAGE ☐☐☐☐

WHERE I STAYED FOR THE NIGHT/RV:

....

WEATHER:

☐   ☐   ☐

☐   ☐   ☐

TEMPERATURE: ....

PEOPLE I MET: ....

....

....

THINGS I WILL REMEMBER:

....

....

....

PLACES THAT I VISITED:

WRITE THE PLACE NUMBERS
FOR EACH LOCATION VISITED

◯ ◯ ◯ ◯

◯ ◯ ◯ ◯

◯ ◯ ◯ ◯

◯ ◯ ◯ ◯

◯ ◯ ◯ ◯

◯ ◯ ◯ ◯

ADDITIONAL PLACES THAT I SAW:

....

....

....

....

DAY NUMBER............ DATE...................

STARTING POINT: .... MILEAGE ☐☐☐☐

ENDING POINT: .... MILEAGE ☐☐☐☐

WHERE I STAYED FOR THE NIGHT/RV:

....

WEATHER:

☐   ☐   ☐

☐   ☐   ☐

🌡 TEMPERATURE: ....

👤 PEOPLE I MET: ....

....

....

THINGS I WILL REMEMBER:

....

....

....

PLACES THAT I VISITED:

WRITE THE PLACE NUMBERS
FOR EACH LOCATION VISITED

◯ ◯ ◯ ◯

◯ ◯ ◯ ◯

◯ ◯ ◯ ◯

◯ ◯ ◯ ◯

◯ ◯ ◯ ◯

◯ ◯ ◯ ◯

ADDITIONAL PLACES THAT I SAW:

....

....

....

....

DAY NUMBER .... DATE ....

STARTING POINT: .... MILEAGE ☐☐☐☐

ENDING POINT: .... MILEAGE ☐☐☐☐

WHERE I STAYED FOR THE NIGHT/RV:

....

WEATHER:

☀️ ☐ ☁️ ☐ ⛅ ☐

🌨️ ☐ 🌧️ ☐ ⛈️ ☐

🌡️ TEMPERATURE: ....

👤 PEOPLE I MET: ....

....

....

THINGS I WILL REMEMBER:

....

....

....

PLACES THAT I VISITED:
WRITE THE PLACE NUMBERS
FOR EACH LOCATION VISITED

◯ ◯ ◯ ◯

◯ ◯ ◯ ◯

◯ ◯ ◯ ◯

◯ ◯ ◯ ◯

◯ ◯ ◯ ◯

◯ ◯ ◯ ◯

ADDITIONAL PLACES THAT I SAW:

....

....

....

....

DAY NUMBER.......... DATE..............

STARTING POINT:............................. MILEAGE ☐☐☐☐

ENDING POINT:............................... MILEAGE ☐☐☐☐

WHERE I STAYED FOR THE NIGHT/RV:

....

WEATHER:

☐ ☐ ☐

☐ ☐ ☐

🌡 TEMPERATURE: ....

👤 PEOPLE I MET: ....

....

....

THINGS I WILL REMEMBER:

....

....

....

PLACES THAT I VISITED:
WRITE THE PLACE NUMBERS
FOR EACH LOCATION VISITED

◯ ◯ ◯ ◯

◯ ◯ ◯ ◯

◯ ◯ ◯ ◯

◯ ◯ ◯ ◯

◯ ◯ ◯ ◯

◯ ◯ ◯ ◯

ADDITIONAL PLACES THAT I SAW:

....

....

....

....

DAY NUMBER .... DATE ....

STARTING POINT: .... MILEAGE ☐☐☐☐

ENDING POINT: .... MILEAGE ☐☐☐☐

WHERE I STAYED FOR THE NIGHT/RV:

....

WEATHER:

☐ ☐ ☐

☐ ☐ ☐

🌡 TEMPERATURE: ....

👤 PEOPLE I MET: ....

....

....

THINGS I WILL REMEMBER:

....

....

....

PLACES THAT I VISITED:

WRITE THE PLACE NUMBERS FOR EACH LOCATION VISITED

◯ ◯ ◯ ◯

◯ ◯ ◯ ◯

◯ ◯ ◯ ◯

◯ ◯ ◯ ◯

◯ ◯ ◯ ◯

◯ ◯ ◯ ◯

ADDITIONAL PLACES THAT I SAW:

....

....

....

....

DAY NUMBER............ DATE....................

STARTING POINT: .... MILEAGE ☐☐☐☐

ENDING POINT: .... MILEAGE ☐☐☐☐

WHERE I STAYED FOR THE NIGHT/RV:

....

WEATHER:

☐   ☐   ☐

☐   ☐   ☐

🌡 TEMPERATURE: ....

👤 PEOPLE I MET: ....

....

....

THINGS I WILL REMEMBER:

....

....

....

PLACES THAT I VISITED:
WRITE THE PLACE NUMBERS
FOR EACH LOCATION VISITED

◯ ◯ ◯ ◯

◯ ◯ ◯ ◯

◯ ◯ ◯ ◯

◯ ◯ ◯ ◯

◯ ◯ ◯ ◯

◯ ◯ ◯ ◯

ADDITIONAL PLACES THAT I SAW:

....

....

....

....

DAY NUMBER............ DATE...................

STARTING POINT:............................ MILEAGE ☐☐☐☐

ENDING POINT:.............................. MILEAGE ☐☐☐☐

WHERE I STAYED FOR THE NIGHT/RV:

....

WEATHER:

☐ ☐ ☐

☐ ☐ ☐

🌡 TEMPERATURE: ....

👤 PEOPLE I MET: ....

....

....

THINGS I WILL REMEMBER:

....

....

....

PLACES THAT I VISITED:

WRITE THE PLACE NUMBERS
FOR EACH LOCATION VISITED

◯ ◯ ◯ ◯

◯ ◯ ◯ ◯

◯ ◯ ◯ ◯

◯ ◯ ◯ ◯

◯ ◯ ◯ ◯

◯ ◯ ◯ ◯

ADDITIONAL PLACES THAT I SAW:

....

....

....

....

DAY NUMBER .... DATE ....

STARTING POINT: .... MILEAGE ☐☐☐☐

ENDING POINT: .... MILEAGE ☐☐☐☐

WHERE I STAYED FOR THE NIGHT/RV:

....

WEATHER:

☐ ☐ ☐

☐ ☐ ☐

TEMPERATURE: ....

PEOPLE I MET: ....

....

....

THINGS I WILL REMEMBER:

....

....

....

PLACES THAT I VISITED:

WRITE THE PLACE NUMBERS
FOR EACH LOCATION VISITED

◯ ◯ ◯ ◯

◯ ◯ ◯ ◯

◯ ◯ ◯ ◯

◯ ◯ ◯ ◯

◯ ◯ ◯ ◯

◯ ◯ ◯ ◯

ADDITIONAL PLACES THAT I SAW:

....

....

....

....

DAY NUMBER.......... DATE....................

STARTING POINT: .... MILEAGE ☐☐☐☐

ENDING POINT: .... MILEAGE ☐☐☐☐

WHERE I STAYED FOR THE NIGHT/RV:

....

WEATHER:

☐ ☐ ☐

☐ ☐ ☐

TEMPERATURE: ....

PEOPLE I MET: ....

....

....

THINGS I WILL REMEMBER:

....

....

....

PLACES THAT I VISITED:
WRITE THE PLACE NUMBERS
FOR EACH LOCATION VISITED

◯ ◯ ◯ ◯

◯ ◯ ◯ ◯

◯ ◯ ◯ ◯

◯ ◯ ◯ ◯

◯ ◯ ◯ ◯

◯ ◯ ◯ ◯

ADDITIONAL PLACES THAT I SAW:

....

....

....

....

DAY NUMBER........... DATE.....................

STARTING POINT: .... MILEAGE ☐☐☐☐

ENDING POINT: .... MILEAGE ☐☐☐☐

WHERE I STAYED FOR THE NIGHT/RV:

....

WEATHER:

☐ ☐ ☐

☐ ☐ ☐

TEMPERATURE: ....

PEOPLE I MET: ....

....

....

THINGS I WILL REMEMBER:

....

....

....

PLACES THAT I VISITED:
WRITE THE PLACE NUMBERS
FOR EACH LOCATION VISITED

◯ ◯ ◯ ◯

◯ ◯ ◯ ◯

◯ ◯ ◯ ◯

◯ ◯ ◯ ◯

◯ ◯ ◯ ◯

◯ ◯ ◯ ◯

ADDITIONAL PLACES THAT I SAW:

....

....

....

....

DAY NUMBER......... DATE...............

STARTING POINT: .... MILEAGE ☐☐☐☐

ENDING POINT: .... MILEAGE ☐☐☐☐

WHERE I STAYED FOR THE NIGHT/RV:

....

WEATHER:

☐   ☐   ☐

☐   ☐   ☐

🌡 TEMPERATURE: ....

👤 PEOPLE I MET: ....

....

....

THINGS I WILL REMEMBER:

....

....

....

PLACES THAT I VISITED:

WRITE THE PLACE NUMBERS
FOR EACH LOCATION VISITED

◯ ◯ ◯ ◯

◯ ◯ ◯ ◯

◯ ◯ ◯ ◯

◯ ◯ ◯ ◯

◯ ◯ ◯ ◯

◯ ◯ ◯ ◯

ADDITIONAL PLACES THAT I SAW:

....

....

....

....

DAY NUMBER.......... DATE..................

STARTING POINT:............................... MILEAGE ☐☐☐☐

ENDING POINT:................................. MILEAGE ☐☐☐☐

WHERE I STAYED FOR THE NIGHT/RV:

....

WEATHER:

☐ ☐ ☐

☐ ☐ ☐

🌡 TEMPERATURE: ....

👤 PEOPLE I MET: ....

....

....

THINGS I WILL REMEMBER:

....

....

....

PLACES THAT I VISITED:

WRITE THE PLACE NUMBERS
FOR EACH LOCATION VISITED

◯ ◯ ◯ ◯

◯ ◯ ◯ ◯

◯ ◯ ◯ ◯

◯ ◯ ◯ ◯

◯ ◯ ◯ ◯

◯ ◯ ◯ ◯

ADDITIONAL PLACES THAT I SAW:

....

....

....

....

DAY NUMBER.......... DATE..................

STARTING POINT:.............................. MILEAGE ☐☐☐☐

ENDING POINT:............................... MILEAGE ☐☐☐☐

WHERE I STAYED FOR THE NIGHT/RV:

....

WEATHER:

☐ ☐ ☐

☐ ☐ ☐

TEMPERATURE: ....

PEOPLE I MET: ....

....

....

THINGS I WILL REMEMBER:

....

....

....

PLACES THAT I VISITED:
WRITE THE PLACE NUMBERS
FOR EACH LOCATION VISITED

◯ ◯ ◯ ◯

◯ ◯ ◯ ◯

◯ ◯ ◯ ◯

◯ ◯ ◯ ◯

◯ ◯ ◯ ◯

◯ ◯ ◯ ◯

ADDITIONAL PLACES THAT I SAW:

....

....

....

....

DAY NUMBER.......... DATE..........

STARTING POINT:..................... MILEAGE ☐☐☐☐

ENDING POINT:..................... MILEAGE ☐☐☐☐

WHERE I STAYED FOR THE NIGHT/RV:

....

WEATHER:

☀️ ☐   ☁️ ☐   ⛅ ☐

❄️ ☐   🌧️ ☐   ⛈️ ☐

🌡️ TEMPERATURE: ....

👤 PEOPLE I MET: ....

....

....

THINGS I WILL REMEMBER:

....

....

....

PLACES THAT I VISITED:

WRITE THE PLACE NUMBERS
FOR EACH LOCATION VISITED

◯ ◯ ◯ ◯

◯ ◯ ◯ ◯

◯ ◯ ◯ ◯

◯ ◯ ◯ ◯

◯ ◯ ◯ ◯

◯ ◯ ◯ ◯

ADDITIONAL PLACES THAT I SAW:

....

....

....

....

DAY NUMBER......... DATE.............

STARTING POINT:.............................. MILEAGE ☐☐☐☐

ENDING POINT:.................................. MILEAGE ☐☐☐☐

WHERE I STAYED FOR THE NIGHT/RV:

....

WEATHER:

☼ ☐   ☁ ☐   ⛅ ☐

❄ ☐   🌧 ☐   ⛈ ☐

🌡 TEMPERATURE: ....

👤 PEOPLE I MET: ....

....

....

THINGS I WILL REMEMBER:

....

....

....

PLACES THAT I VISITED:
WRITE THE PLACE NUMBERS
FOR EACH LOCATION VISITED

◯ ◯ ◯ ◯

◯ ◯ ◯ ◯

◯ ◯ ◯ ◯

◯ ◯ ◯ ◯

◯ ◯ ◯ ◯

◯ ◯ ◯ ◯

ADDITIONAL PLACES THAT I SAW:

....

....

....

....

DAY NUMBER .... DATE ....

STARTING POINT: .... MILEAGE ☐☐☐☐

ENDING POINT: .... MILEAGE ☐☐☐☐

WHERE I STAYED FOR THE NIGHT/RV:

....

WEATHER:

☐ ☐ ☐

☐ ☐ ☐

TEMPERATURE: ....

PEOPLE I MET: ....

....

....

THINGS I WILL REMEMBER:

....

....

....

PLACES THAT I VISITED:

WRITE THE PLACE NUMBERS
FOR EACH LOCATION VISITED

◯ ◯ ◯ ◯

◯ ◯ ◯ ◯

◯ ◯ ◯ ◯

◯ ◯ ◯ ◯

◯ ◯ ◯ ◯

◯ ◯ ◯ ◯

ADDITIONAL PLACES THAT I SAW:

....

....

....

....

DAY NUMBER......... DATE...............

STARTING POINT:.............................. MILEAGE ☐☐☐☐

ENDING POINT:................................. MILEAGE ☐☐☐☐

WHERE I STAYED FOR THE NIGHT/RV:

....

WEATHER:

☐ ☐ ☐

☐ ☐ ☐

🌡 TEMPERATURE: ....

👤 PEOPLE I MET: ....

....

....

THINGS I WILL REMEMBER:

....

....

....

PLACES THAT I VISITED:
WRITE THE PLACE NUMBERS FOR EACH LOCATION VISITED

◯ ◯ ◯ ◯

◯ ◯ ◯ ◯

◯ ◯ ◯ ◯

◯ ◯ ◯ ◯

◯ ◯ ◯ ◯

◯ ◯ ◯ ◯

ADDITIONAL PLACES THAT I SAW:

....

....

....

....

DAY NUMBER......... DATE........

STARTING POINT: .... MILEAGE ☐☐☐☐

ENDING POINT: .... MILEAGE ☐☐☐☐

WHERE I STAYED FOR THE NIGHT/RV:

....

WEATHER:

☐ ☐ ☐

☐ ☐ ☐

🌡 TEMPERATURE: ....

👤 PEOPLE I MET: ....

....

....

THINGS I WILL REMEMBER:

....

....

....

PLACES THAT I VISITED:

WRITE THE PLACE NUMBERS
FOR EACH LOCATION VISITED

○ ○ ○ ○

○ ○ ○ ○

○ ○ ○ ○

○ ○ ○ ○

○ ○ ○ ○

○ ○ ○ ○

ADDITIONAL PLACES THAT I SAW:

....

....

....

....

DAY NUMBER.......... DATE..................

STARTING POINT: .... MILEAGE ☐☐☐☐

ENDING POINT: .... MILEAGE ☐☐☐☐

WHERE I STAYED FOR THE NIGHT/RV:

....

WEATHER:

☐   ☐   ☐

☐   ☐   ☐

TEMPERATURE: ....

PEOPLE I MET: ....

....

....

THINGS I WILL REMEMBER:

....

....

....

PLACES THAT I VISITED:
WRITE THE PLACE NUMBERS
FOR EACH LOCATION VISITED

◯ ◯ ◯ ◯

◯ ◯ ◯ ◯

◯ ◯ ◯ ◯

◯ ◯ ◯ ◯

◯ ◯ ◯ ◯

◯ ◯ ◯ ◯

ADDITIONAL PLACES THAT I SAW:

....

....

....

....

NOTES:

NOTES:

....

....

....

....

....

....

....

....

....

....

....

....

....

NOTES:

AUTHOR: MARK WATSON
GRAPHIC DESIGN: BART TROCH
EDITOR: RUSS L.
COPYRIGHT 2024
LOS ANGELES CA. U.S.A

Made in the USA
Las Vegas, NV
28 February 2024